SPORTS HEROES AND LEGENDS™

Ichiro Suzuki

Read all of the books in this exciting,
action-packed biography series!

Barry Bonds

Ichiro Suzuki

Lou Gehrig

Michelle Kwan

Mickey Mantle

Tim Duncan

Ichiro Suzuki

by David S. Leigh

LERNER
SPORTS
AN IMPRINT OF LERNER PUBLISHING GROUP

*For my sweeters—your support means the world to me.
And thanks to Bryan, the baseball guru.*

Copyright © 2004 by Lerner Publications Company

Sports Heroes and Legends™ is a trademark of Barnes and Noble.

Used with permission from Barnes and Noble.

LernerSports
An imprint of Lerner Publishing Group
241 First Avenue North
Minneapolis, MN 55401 U.S.A.

Website address: www.lernerbooks.com

Cover photograph:
© Rob Tringali/SportsChrome

Library of Congress Cataloging-in-Publication Data

Leigh, David S., 1970–
   Ichiro Suzuki / by David S. Leigh.
       p.   cm. — (Sports heroes and legends)
     Contents: East meets West—For the love of the game—Practice makes perfect—Going pro—One-name wonder—Ichiromania—Time for change—Dream come true — Making wave—Playing it cool—Here to stay.
     ISBN: 0–8225–1792–2 (lib. bdg. : alk. paper)
     1. Suzuki, Ichiro, 1973—Juvenile literature. 2. Baseball players—Japan—Biography—Juvenile literature. [1. Suzuki, Ichiro, 1973–
2. Baseball players. 3. Japanese—Washington (State)—Biography.]
I. Title. II. Series.
GV865.S895L45 2004
796.357′092—dc22   2003025882

Manufactured in the United States of America
1 2 3 4 5 6 – JR – 09 08 07 06 05 04

Contents

Prologue
Hitting for History
1

Chapter One
East Meets West
5

Chapter Two
For the Love of the Game
15

Chapter Three
Practice Makes Perfect
21

Chapter Four
Going Pro
27

Chapter Five
One-Name Wonder
34

Chapter Six
Ichiromania
41

Chapter Seven
Time for Change
51

Chapter Eight
Dream Come True
59

Chapter Nine
Making Waves
70

Chapter Ten
Playing It Cool
81

Chapter Eleven
Here to Stay
87

Epilogue
A Bright Future
93

Personal Statistics
96

Batting Statistics (Japan)
97

Batting Statistics (U.S.)
97

Fielding Statistics (Japan)
98

Fielding Statistics [U.S.]
98

Sources
99

Bibliography
102

Websites
104

Index
105

Hitting for History

I chiro (ee-chee-ro) Suzuki had a lot at stake when he walked onto the grass at Safeco Field in Seattle, Washington, on April 2, 2001. On his first day as a Seattle Mariner, fans across the globe were watching to see what this much-hailed baseball star from Japan would do.

Ichiro was a baseball king in his homeland, and some of his Japanese fans had flown halfway across the world to witness their hero's debut as a U.S. major leaguer. Even more impressive, twelve million fans were watching him on television in Japan, where it was 11:15 AM on a workday. For them, it was no ordinary game!

The twenty-seven-year-old outfielder was making history as the first Japanese position player (nonpitcher) to make the leap to the American major leagues. Ichiro, as he was known, had risen to fame in Japan as an All-Star outfielder with Japan's

1

Orix Blue Wave team. He knew fans would be studying every move he made in the debut game. For someone without his focus, it could have been overwhelming. Ichiro had his most important fan in the audience, his father, Nobuyuki Suzuki, who was perched in a first-row seat behind the Mariners' dugout, proud and anxious to see how his son would perform.

At 7:15 PM Seattle time, Ichiro stepped up to the batter's box at the bottom of the first inning to face Oakland A's pitcher Tim Hudson. Flashbulbs went off in the press area, where the Japanese reporters and photographers, along with eager American sportswriters, were ready to document his every move.

On the second pitch, Ichiro slapped a hopping grounder to second base. He sprinted to first, but Oakland's second baseman, Jose Ortiz, caught the ball and tossed it to first for an out. Even though he'd been thrown out, Ichiro was pleased. He'd just made his first play as a U.S. major leaguer!

Ichiro didn't fare much better in his next two at bats—he was tagged out again in the third and struck out in the fifth. His next chance came in the seventh inning. The A's were ahead 4–2. Relief pitcher T. J. Mathews aimed a fastball at Ichiro, who smashed it up the middle. The ball bounced into center field, and Ichiro safely made it to first. The crowd went wild, as did fans across Japan.

Once on base, Ichiro used his reputation as a top-notch base stealer to his advantage. Mathews was so concerned with keeping Ichiro from sneaking to the next base that he had trouble focusing on his pitches. He walked the next batter, Mike Cameron, and Ichiro advanced to second. The A's started feeling nervous, and they replaced Mathews with Jim Mecir. When the next batter, Edgar Martinez, knocked out a single, Ichiro raced around the bases, scoring his first run. The excitement increasing, Mariner John Olerud hit another single, allowing Cameron to score and tie up the game.

In the eighth inning, Ichiro could feel the pressure. Mariner Carlos Guillen had just reached first base on a walk, and the game was still tied at 4–4. Instead of smacking the ball, which the A's expected, Ichiro bunted the ball down the first-base line. The infield scrambled for the ball, and a frantic throw to first was off the mark. First baseman Jason Giambi missed the catch, allowing Ichiro to speed to second base and Guillen to make it safely to third.

Two batters later, Olerud hit a long sacrifice fly to the outfield, bringing Guillen in and giving the Mariners the lead. In the top of the ninth, Mariners relief pitcher Kazuhiro Sasaki, a former opponent of Ichiro's in Japan, took the mound and didn't allow a single run, sealing up the game for the Mariners.

After the game was over, Ichiro told reporters, "A few years

3

ago, Kazuhiro talked about how great it would be to play on the same team, to have a good game and then have Kazu come in and save it. To have all that in our very first game is unbelievable."

But to some, even more unbelievable was the fact that in his very first game, Ichiro proved that a Japanese position player could hold his own in the U.S. major leagues. He single-handedly silenced the critics who had claimed a Japanese hitter wouldn't be able to measure up to the power of American pitchers. Not only was Ichiro able to handle whatever was thrown his way, he was going to give the U.S. major-league players some serious competition!

Chapter One

East Meets West

Long before Ichiro began playing baseball, the sport had been established as one of the most popular pastimes in Japan. Horace Wilson, an American professor teaching at the Kaisei Gakko school in Tokyo, Japan's capital city, first introduced baseball to his students in the 1870s. At that time, Japan was in the Meiji era (1867–1912), a period of social, cultural, and technological innovation to catch up to the United States and Europe. To build up its industry, Japan brought in Western experts. Some of these teachers-in-residence introduced Western culture, including baseball, to their eager students.

At first the Western game of baseball was a curiosity to the Japanese students. They took to it quickly, however, and the game, which the Japanese called *yakyu,* or "field ball," began steadily gaining in popularity.

Although many Americans consider baseball to be 100

percent American, the game is, in a sense, tailor-made for Japan. The sport's focus on the one-on-one battle between pitcher and batter and its blend of mental and physical strength are similar to aspects of martial arts and sumo wrestling, both extremely popular in Japan.

Hiroshi Hiraoka, a railroad engineer who had left Japan to study in Boston, Massachusetts, for several years, is credited with forming Japan's first baseball team, the Shimbashi Athletic Club Athletics, in 1883. For the most part, those involved with the amateur club worked for the Japanese railroad, which ran from Shimbashi in Tokyo to the port of Yokohama. They played against university teams as well as private clubs like the Yokohama Country Club baseball team.

On a larger scale, the Japanese Ministry of Education encouraged students to play baseball. It was seen as the perfect bridge between Eastern and Western culture. The ministry believed baseball's mixture of strategy and physical ability would be good for the character of the Japanese people.

Apart from the Shimbashi team, baseball first became popular in the Japanese school system, especially at the high school and college levels. Baseball caught on like wildfire and an annual high school baseball tournament, called Koshien, was established. Those who played baseball were in for a rigorous workout. Coaches and managers pushed their young players to

6

the limit, making them endure long hours of practice to fine-tune their form, hone their pitches, and perfect their swings.

CAMPAIGN AGAINST BASEBALL

In the early 1900s, the *Asahi Shimbun,* a conservative Japanese newspaper, ran a series of articles called "The Evil of Baseball." Among its claims were that the "mental pressure" of baseball was bad for personality development and that the body could become lopsided from throwing a baseball.

With their intense training, Japanese baseball teams began rapidly improving their game. Matsutaro Shoriki, a newspaper owner, became known as the "great genius-father figure" of baseball after coming up with the idea to have American baseball players tour Japan to play against local Japanese players in 1908. For the first time, Japanese ballplayers were exposed to the skills of their Western counterparts. In 1913 the Chicago White Sox played four games in Japan, and as time went by, other teams followed. Although the Japanese players trained extremely hard, they did not fare well in these early matchups against American teams.

By the early 1920s, the first professional Japanese baseball club, the Shibaura Club, was founded. A decade later, in 1934, the *Yomiuri Shimbun,* a leading newspaper, organized another team, the Dai Nippon (renamed the Yomiuri Giants the following year).

The *Yomiuri Shimbun* formed its team after a visit from New York Yankees legend Babe Ruth, who traveled to Japan with some fellow major leaguers to play a series of exhibition games. Ruth gave Japanese baseball fans a taste of his amazing talent. In seventeen sold-out games (all of which the Americans won), he batted .408 and scored thirteen home runs. The Babe's presence created quite a stir and gave the country a huge boost in its fascination with the game.

In 1936 six Japanese businesses followed the example of the *Yomiuri Shimbun* and established baseball teams of their own. The companies sponsoring the teams generally owned newspapers or train lines. The newspapers hoped to boost circulation by attaching their name to a team, and the train owners wanted people to travel on their trains to see their teams play. These teams—the Yomiuri Giants, the Osaka Tigers, Hankyu, Dai Tokyo, Nagoya Kinko, Nagoya, and the Tokyo Senators—made up the Japanese Professional Baseball League.

But with the expansion of World War II in 1941, life changed drastically in Japan. Japan and America became enemies after the surprise attack on the American naval base at Pearl Harbor on December 7, 1941. Later in the war, America dropped atomic bombs on the Japanese cities of Hiroshima and Nagasaki. Japan's favorite pastime, which had become a national craze, took a backseat to the conflict. Baseball games were suspended because so many men had enlisted in the military. Stadiums that had once been filled with devoted baseball fans were torn down to provide more land for crops or ammunition storage. Interestingly, even though baseball had been invented in America, there was no anti-baseball backlash, despite the fact that there was anti-American sentiment in Japan at the time. After all, Japan had at this point fully adopted the game as its own.

After the war was over and the Japanese surrendered to the Americans in 1945, the Allied forces—led by U.S. commander General Douglas MacArthur—occupied Japan. MacArthur felt that baseball would be a good way to reinvigorate Japan and boost the country's morale. Within nine months of the beginning of the Allied occupation, Japan's pro leagues were up and running.

To show that the country was renewing its spirit and moving past the tragedy of World War II, American soldiers built a baseball stadium across the street from where the atomic bomb had been dropped in Hiroshima. "Baseball was a big part of that country coming back together," baseball scout Ted Heid said. "Our armed forces rebuilt fields right away. Our servicemen liked it because they could play, and it was a chance for Americans and Japanese to play against each other."

After World War II, the Japanese established their own baseball terminology. *Pitcher* was *toshu, first base* was *ichirui, hitter* was *dasha,* and so on.

As life in Japan began settling back to normal, baseball became a permanent fixture in the country. In 1950 the Japan Professional Baseball League split into two leagues, the Central and Pacific. Each league had six teams. The teams from the original 1936 league were divided between the two leagues, and new teams were founded. In 1951, when a U.S. exhibition team came to play against the Japanese All-Stars, the country rejoiced to see their players beat the visiting Americans. The Japanese were also thrilled when American baseball stars such as Joe DiMaggio made their way to their country.

By 1955 the advent of television was also helping the game grow. People who weren't able to get out to the stadiums could watch their favorite teams at home. In 1962 the first American players began playing professionally in Japan. The Americans, who traditionally came to Japan to play in the final years of their career, were referred to as *gaijin,* or foreigners. The Japanese league limited how many foreigners could play on a given team, typically no more than two.

In 1964 the first Japanese players traveled to join American teams. To educate their players in the ways of American baseball, the Nankai Hawks sent three players to spend time in the minor leagues. One of them, pitcher Masanori Murakami, played for a Class A Fresno farm team and was then called up to play for the major-league San Francisco Giants. In 1965 he pitched nearly fifty major-league games. Partway through the season, he returned home after a disagreement between the Giants and the Hawks over who had the rights to his career.

At that time, Japan's top baseball team was the Yomiuri Giants, who scored nine consecutive Japan Series championships from 1965 to 1973. (The Japan Series is the equivalent of the World Series, in which the top teams from the two leagues play each other in a final postseason seven-game series.)

Players who traveled between the United States and Japan noticed a variety of differences between the American game and the Japanese game. American players who joined Japanese teams were shocked by the length and intensity of practices.

11

The grueling practices occur even on game and travel days, unlike in the United States. "In Japan, a good hard workout every day is considered imperative in order to show the fans, the press, and the opposition that the team is full of fight," journalist Toni Hassan explained in an interview about Japanese baseball.

If you think baseball players in America train hard, think again. It was once said in Japan that if players weren't bleeding, they weren't practicing hard enough.

In Japan teamwork is king. From the time Japanese ballplayers are young, they learn that it's more important to play for team success than individual glory. Sacrifice bunting is encouraged if it will help the next player get to bat. While hitting a home run is key in America, "[in Japan] you have to sacrifice for the good of your team," sportswriter Jim Allen told *Time* magazine.

The Japanese game also has a few unique rules. For example, a fan who catches a foul ball cannot keep it—in most stadiums, the custom is that the ball must be returned to the usher, supposedly for the safety of the fan. If a game is tied after twelve innings, it must end in a tie. It's also common for a game to end between 10:15 and 10:30 PM even if it hasn't reached a full nine innings. This custom is observed so that fans and even players can make their way home on public transportation. Most stadiums, which are near Tokyo or Osaka, don't even have parking lots.

Until the mid-1990s, Japanese pitchers were widely considered not as fast or strong as their American counterparts. In 1995 Hideo Nomo became the first Japanese player since Murakami to make it to the U.S. majors. When he joined the Los Angeles Dodgers, he began a new chapter for Japanese players hoping to make their mark in the United States. Following him were pitchers Hideki Irabu, who joined the New York Yankees in 1997, and Kazuhiro Sasaki, who joined the Seattle Mariners in 1999. Nomo continues to have success with the Dodgers. Irabu, who was traded to the Texas Rangers, returned to Japan after six uneven seasons as a U.S. major leaguer. Meanwhile, Sasaki has flourished and remains a star relief pitcher for the Mariners.

❝I feel comfortable here. Pitchers challenge hitters: power against power. The way they play in America is the way I feel the game should be played.❞
—SEATTLE MARINERS RELIEF PITCHER KAZUHIRO SASAKI

Even though these pitchers attracted a lot of attention in the major leagues, no Japanese position player had made the transition. Many U.S. scouts and coaches thought that Japanese hitters couldn't handle the speed of American pitchers and that the Japanese style of playing wouldn't work in the big leagues. "When you watch a hitter in Japan, his abilities are discounted because [people] say he's not hitting against major-league pitching," said former New York Mets manager Bobby Valentine, who managed Japan's Chiba Lotte Marines in 1995.

Unlike pitchers, who could still pitch approximately the same number of games in the United States as in Japan, position players face a longer season—162 games compared to 140. Japanese players who come to America also face more travel and have to get used to a wider variety of pitchers. Overcoming these obstacles was a huge challenge for a Japanese position player hoping to be successful in the United States.

It would take a skilled, focused player to make his mark on the American major leagues. The player to fill that void would be Ichiro Suzuki.

Chapter | Two

For the Love of the Game

Ichiro Suzuki was born on October 22, 1973, in the Aichi prefecture (which is similar to a state or a province) of Japan. The son of Yoshie, his mom, and Nobuyuki, his dad, he grew up in the town of Toyoyama, a suburb of the city of Nagoya, which is 150 miles southwest of Tokyo. Ichiro had baseball in his blood from the very beginning. His father was a fervent fan of the game, and his favorite team was Nagoya's home team, the Chunichi Dragons.

Nobuyuki, who ran his own business, had played baseball in high school but didn't have the talent to take his career further. When Ichiro was only three years old, his father gave him a baseball glove and a ball so that he could learn to throw and catch. "The glove wasn't a toy, but a real glove made of red leather. I was so excited about getting it I carried it everywhere," Ichiro recalled.

At age six, as a first grader, Ichiro decided he wanted to play on the local Little League team at the Toyoyama Children's Sports Club. The only problem was his age. A boy had to be in at least third grade to join. That wasn't about to stop him. Despite the fact that Ichiro's small size was a giveaway that he was underage, his determination and skill at both batting and fielding won out and the club allowed him to join. "I managed to talk my way in," he recalled. It also helped that his father was the Little League team's coach.

Ichiro's father was very serious about teaching him how to play and groomed him to be an athlete in every way. He wouldn't allow Ichiro to eat any junk food. Ice cream and candy were out. The whole family was involved in helping Ichiro grow big and strong. Ichiro's aunt even made him a soup with special muscle-building ingredients. Ichiro gulped down the soup all the time.

❝Nobody else practiced the way I did, every day.❞
—ICHIRO

Despite the fact that the team only practiced on Sundays, Ichiro and his father still practiced hitting and fielding daily. Father and son would head together to the neighborhood fields, the Iseyama grounds, down the street from their home. They'd run from the house to the park to get their hearts racing, and once they were there, they would do warm-up exercises. Then they'd practice pitching and batting, and at the end, Ichiro would shag fly balls.

Occasionally battles would break out between headstrong Ichiro and his father, who was a tough taskmaster and demanded a lot from his young son. If Ichiro wanted to end practice early to watch a show on television, that would cause a quarrel. To teach him responsibility, Nobuyuki had Ichiro carry all the equipment to and from the field. "Sometimes it was pretty hard to take. . . . He says it was all sweetness and light," Ichiro has said of his father's memory of their practice sessions. "But it wasn't that nice."

It was a tough, no-nonsense way to learn the sport. Yet there were happy moments as well, like when the pair would go to Nagoya Stadium to see their favorite team, the Dragons, play. Or when after their practices, his father would massage the soles of Ichiro's feet, which helped to relax his whole body. That became a part of their daily routine.

Ichiro's intense training was paying off because he was rapidly becoming a stellar batter and pitcher. Although he was right-handed, his father encouraged him to start batting left-handed because he felt that with Ichiro's speed, hitting lefty would be the way to go. He'd be that much closer to first base!

Ichiro, ever the quick study, adapted to that switch pretty quickly and was soon hitting left-handed like a natural.

❝*I think I was in third or fourth grade when I started seeing [baseball] as my real dream for the future.*❞
—Ichiro

By the time he was in third grade, Ichiro was clearly far ahead in his skills compared to his schoolmates. While his friends were learning the basics of baseball, Ichiro was finding his father's pitches too easy. He needed more of a challenge.

When he was in fifth grade, Ichiro and his father began going to the local batting center, where he hit sixty-mile-per-hour pitches. Batters twice and three times his age would stand in amazement as they watched the pint-size player hit pitch after pitch with great dexterity. Word began spreading about this phenomenal young player.

Ichiro also benefited from his father's adventurous style of coaching. Nobuyuki would encourage him to imitate players he saw on TV. At an early age, Ichiro developed a one-legged swinging stance that he based on the style of Kazunori Shinozuka, a power hitter for the Yomiuri Giants. As the pitcher wound up for the throw, Ichiro lifted his front leg and swung it like a long, slow pendulum back toward the catcher. He was in essence balancing on one foot as the pitch came toward him. In the final moments, he'd swing his bat around with blinding speed.

Though Ichiro was inspired by Japanese ballplayers in developing his swing, Ichiro's dad has said that he was also inspired by the golf swing of female pro golfer Ayako Okamoto.

In his pitching—a skill that impressed his fellow teammates and coaches at an early age—Ichiro was influenced by Tatsuo Komatsu, who played for the Chunichi Dragons. "When I pitched like Komatsu did, bringing the ball down sharply, I was able to put a lot behind the pitch, and my own form gradually changed because of this," Ichiro recalled.

When Ichiro reached junior high school, he would practice daily with his teammates on the Toyoyama Junior High School team. His father was there for his games and was sure to tell him if he had done something wrong. When a game or practice was over, Ichiro and his dad would head to the batting cages, where Ichiro was hitting eighty-mile-per-hour pitches. The batting center had to install a special spring into the machine to make it fast enough for young Ichiro! Nobuyuki had to call ahead to get the machine set up before they'd go to the batting cages because no one else could bat at that speed. Ichiro was becoming a local celebrity.

One time young Ichiro batted at the cages with a well-known high school cleanup batter, and it became quickly apparent to Ichiro that despite the age difference, he was as good, if not better, than the older boy. As he developed as a batter, his pitching skills were also rapidly improving. Ichiro was developing a keen fastball. He helped his school to a third-place finish in the national tournament, and his arm was becoming quite an obstacle against opposing teams' batters.

By the end of junior high, baseball was everything to Ichiro. It was time for him—and his classmates—to take high school entrance exams. Scoring well would enable him to have his pick of high schools. Although Ichiro was a good student, he knew the school's baseball team would be the main factor in his decision. "I wanted to go to one of those schools with a competitive team," he recalled. Ichiro was more than ready to take his game to the next level.

Chapter Three

Practice Makes Perfect

After taking his high school entrance exams and getting accepted to several schools, Ichiro chose to enter the Aiko-Dai Meiden High School. Eleven Aiko-Dai players had already been sent to the Japanese pros. It seemed like the perfect match. Because of the school's distance from his home in Toyoyama, Ichiro would have to stay in a dormitory.

On Ichiro's first day of baseball practice, the team's manager, Go Nakamura, got his first glimpse of Ichiro. He found it hard to believe that this small kid had the kind of skills that had people raving. "When Mr. Nakamura first saw me, apparently he said, 'How can someone this scrawny play ball?'" Ichiro recalled.

Nakamura soon saw that his first impression was all wrong. Despite Ichiro's slight appearance, this serious-minded perfectionist was all business when it came to his game. "He was something else when it came to his power of concentration.

Even in practice, he didn't take his time. He was the type who would quickly focus on the task and get it done," Nakamura said.

But Ichiro would have more challenges than just convincing people that he could play ball. He was forced to show his mettle off the field. Freshmen and sophomore players had the task of catering to the junior and senior athletes, who basically ruled the school. Japanese society as a whole emphasizes respect for elders, so Ichiro and his fellow younger players had no choice but to obey the upperclassmen.

❝ *Mr. Nakamura told me when I entered the school, 'For the rest of your life you'll never experience anything as tough as what you're going to go through now.'* **❞**
— ICHIRO ON HIS HIGH SCHOOL DAYS

Occasionally Ichiro would be punished by one of the senior athletes for cooking rice badly or some other small error. They would force him to kneel on the lid of a garbage can until they felt he had been punished long enough. "Once I remember they caught me eating a soft ice-cream cone I'd gone out to buy and it was up on the garbage can for me," Ichiro remembered with a laugh about the payback for sneaking out to get a treat.

Regardless of the paces he was put through, Ichiro didn't let anything stop him from practicing—however and whenever

22

he could. Because priority was given to the seniors in the indoor batting cage or in the gym, Ichiro had to be creative in finding other methods of working on his skills. He'd run laps, swing his bat on the tennis courts—do anything he could to stay sharp and in shape. He knew that practicing hard would help him do his best on the field.

Much of Ichiro's free time after dinner was spent at the washing machines and dryers, doing laundry for the upperclassmen (and for himself). This was time he would rather have spent practicing, so he came up with a solution. He began waking up at 3 AM to do the laundry while everyone else slept. Of course, that meant that Ichiro got only several hours of sleep every night.

As the year went on, Ichiro was becoming a mighty pitcher. He became known for delivering tricky pitches to opposing teams. When he took the field, his opponents knew they were in for a tough time. Yet the budding pitcher's dreams almost came to an end when a car knocked him off his bicycle during his sophomore year, causing a contusion in his right calf. After a month on crutches, Ichiro returned to the team but could not endure the intensity of pitching while he was healing. He was switched to first base, which required less constant throwing, while he was on the mend. But the time away proved detrimental to Ichiro's pitching arm.

"Tossing the ball from first to second or third is completely different from the way a pitcher throws. While I was playing first, I got used to throwing [the ball] the way a fielder does, so when I tried again to throw it like a pitcher, the alignment of my arm was out of whack and I hit myself on the head with the ball before it even left my hand," Ichiro commented. "Once you've picked up the wrong form, it's really hard to change back."

If high school students in the United States think they spend too much time in school, they should look at their Japanese counterparts. While Americans spend 180 days a year in school, Japanese kids attend classes a whopping 240 days a year. The school year begins in April and consists of three terms, separated by short holidays in the spring and winter and a one-month summer break.

Ichiro wasn't discouraged or deterred. After all, he had as much passion for running and hitting as he did for pitching, so he put his efforts into improving his running and hitting even more. During the summer of his sophomore year, Ichiro and his team made it to Koshien, the famed national high school tournament. Fewer than fifty teams from more than 3,000 high school teams make it to the tournament. Koshien takes place twice a year, in the spring and summer, and is held in Koshien Stadium. It is immensely popular with baseball fans of all ages.

Ichiro knew Koshien was a chance to get national attention and have pro baseball scouts take notice of him. He wanted to make the most of his time at the tournament. Unfortunately, his team lost right away and didn't make it past the first round. Although the loss could have been a huge disappointment to Ichiro, he wasn't that sad about it. Instead, he was doubly determined to make it back the following year.

He got his wish. By his junior year, Ichiro had evolved into a star upperclassman player at Aiko-Dai. After recovering from his sophomore-year injury, he had returned to pitching and was the driving force behind his team's success. They made it back to the spring Koshien tournament, where Ichiro had another chance to make a splash!

When Ichiro was a high school pitcher, his fastball was timed at more than ninety miles per hour.

The game was broadcast live on TV. Ichiro felt a lot of pressure, knowing he was being watched by people all over the country. Again the team lasted just one round before getting eliminated. It was another tough break. Ichiro felt upset that he hadn't quite played up to his potential.

During his senior year, Ichiro proved his abilities time and time again. He was pitching well and hitting with finesse. He was hardly striking out and was handily scoring run after run for his team. By the time the summer regional qualifying tournament for Koshien rolled around, Ichiro was in top form. He knew the tournament would be his prime opportunity to get noticed by the pro scouts. He had one major goal for the tournament: to bat a thousand (1.000). That meant he had to get a hit every time at bat. Could he do it?

In seven games, Ichiro got eighteen hits in twenty-five at bats. He didn't exactly meet his lofty aspiration, but he certainly made the scouts sit up and take notice. His final batting average in the tournament was an impressive .643. Unfortunately, the team was one win shy of making it to Koshien.

Recalled Ichiro, "Everyone on the team was crying, since we'd done our best but still couldn't win the championship. But I soon got over it." That's because he had his eyes on one thing: getting drafted by the pros.

Chapter Four

Going Pro

After graduating from high school in 1991, Ichiro hoped to become a pro baseball player. Professional teams draft many players right after high school graduation, although some also get selected after going to college. Ichiro kept his fingers crossed that he would be picked right away.

In the first round of draft picks, Ichiro wasn't chosen. He wasn't selected in the second or third round either. Ichiro's high school injury and time away from the pitcher's mound had made him a less realistic candidate for a major-league pitching position. His small size (five-foot nine and 150 pounds) also worked against him. Pro teams thought he might not be able to handle the tough demands of being a major-league pitcher.

Ichiro still had strong hitting and fielding skills, which he had showcased at Koshien and in his high school career. These qualities made him a good candidate for a position as an outfielder or infielder. A team just had to be willing to take a chance on him.

In the fourth round of draft picks in November 1991, Ichiro was selected as an outfielder by the Kobe-based Orix Blue Wave. His father, Nobuyuki, who had dreamed of his son being selected by the Chunichi Dragons, was disappointed. Ichiro, on the other hand, was ecstatic. He was finally a pro ballplayer, even though he didn't know much about the Blue Wave. All his hard work was paying off.

NAMING GAME

Unlike in America, Japanese baseball teams aren't identified by the cities in which they play—they're categorized by the company that owns them. The Orix Blue Wave, Ichiro's pro team in Japan, has been owned by Orix, a leasing company, since 1989. Before that they were owned by Hankyu Railways.

Ichiro has a distinct memory of the first time he felt like a real professional. "I was in my room at the Seitokan dorm for single players [in Kobe] and put on my uniform for the first time. I pestered the older players a lot, asking them how they thought I looked in it," he recalled.

One of the team's scouts, Katsutoshi Miwata, became like a second father to Ichiro. He instructed Ichiro to do sit-ups to build his abdominal muscles and gave him other advice. Ichiro was determined to do everything he could to make a good impression as a pro player.

Yet it wasn't an easy transition. He had to overcome the doubts of naysayers who took one look at his size and thought he was too much of a lightweight. One of his biggest doubters was the Blue Wave's manager, Shozo Doi. When Ichiro first arrived at training camp, he thought Ichiro looked like a kid and disliked his unique style of batting.

Ichiro's stance at the plate, in which he kicked his leg high, didn't sit well with Doi, who told him point-blank, "You'll never hit." Ichiro was sent down to the minor leagues.

Yet Ichiro had always had faith in his abilities, and he wasn't about to stop believing in himself. He decided that he would make the most of his time in the minors, improving his skills and learning everything he could. He worked hard, and just a few months into his first season, he was batting over .300.

In July, several months after he signed up with the team, he was called up to Orix's major-league team. But instead of being excited about it, Ichiro was nervous. The nineteen-year-old player had doubts. "I thought I couldn't handle the pitchers at the Japanese major-league level. But in reality I did hit off them," he recalled. In forty games, he hit .253 and didn't make any errors in the outfield. It was a respectable start for the player, who was less than a year out of high school.

But Ichiro wasn't in the majors for long. Soon Doi sent him back down to the minors to get more experience. He flourished. At the end of his first season with the Orix farm team, he hit .366 in fifty-eight games. He was also named Most Valuable Player (MVP) of the minor-league All-Star game.

During that All-Star game, Ichiro had planned to hit the ball to the left side of the infield but looked over to his father in the stands. Nobuyuki signaled to hit the ball to the right. Ichiro took the cue and hit a home run. He later knocked off a single and stole second *and* third base. "I like to steal. I'm good at it," Ichiro told Japan's *Baseball Magazine* after the game. "When I steal third, unlike when it's really close at second, I want to cruise in . . . without sliding, so I can really surprise people." Ichiro's strategy for stealing paid off and he finished the season with the most stolen bases in the minor leagues.

Despite the happy ending to his 1992 season, things weren't so joyous for Ichiro in 1993. He was a bit like a Ping-Pong ball, bouncing back and forth from the majors to the minors several times. He still didn't have a whole lot of support from manager Doi.

Even though Ichiro had done well in the minors, Doi

continued to dislike his swing. Ichiro would stand at the plate, hold the bat straight out in front of him with his right hand, whirl it around, position it over his left shoulder, and shuffle his feet as the pitcher got ready to throw to him. Then came the leg lift. Doi wanted Ichiro to just stand firm in the batter's box and swing, no fancy stuff. Ichiro disagreed. Doi also chided Ichiro for wanting to hit home runs, complaining that he was trying to be too showy. Unlike in America, where coaches place a lot of emphasis on home run hitting, Japanese coaches spend a lot of time on sharpening bunting and baserunning skills. This approach supports their focus on teamwork etiquette rather than trying to make individual stars out of players.

❝*I was thinking, 'What if there was a different coach every year? I'd have to change my style to suit each one of them.' I wouldn't be playing very long if I did that.***❞**
—ICHIRO ON INSISTING ON KEEPING
HIS OWN PERSONAL BATTING STYLE

In a June 12, 1993, game against the Kintetsu Buffaloes, in which Ichiro was pitted against the pitching skills of Hideo Nomo, Ichiro hit a home run. Instead of celebrating Ichiro's success, Orix's coaching staff lectured him to stop showing off.

A palpable friction existed between the manager, who thought his young player was being disrespectful, and Ichiro, who resented being asked to change his hitting style. Doi went into action, putting Ichiro on the bench and only occasionally playing him.

It was a disastrous situation. Ichiro was unhappy and hitting badly. Although he had tried hitting differently to please Doi and the batting coaches, he realized it didn't feel natural. Ichiro felt that the only way he'd have any level of success as a hitter would be by hitting his own way. It was a rebellious decision.

"Near the end of the season our batting coach told me this: 'This is your last chance. If you do what I say, I'll teach you. Otherwise you're on your own.' I made it quite clear I wasn't about to listen to him, and the next day I was sent down to the [minor-league] team. I didn't have the slightest intention of changing my batting form." The Orix batting staff even asked Ichiro's father to intervene on their behalf, which he admitted wouldn't do any good. Ichiro was going to do things on his terms.

Luckily for Ichiro, he had support from Kenichiro Kawamura, the coach for Orix's minor-league squad. Kawamura had faith in Ichiro and his unusual batting style, sensing that it worked well for him both physically and mentally. Ichiro was much happier in the minor leagues because he felt he was valued as a player.

Kawamura worked with Ichiro on his timing as a batter. He also crystallized for Ichiro that hitting wasn't only about the physical act of making contact with the ball. It was also about the mental aspect of batting. "He'd say things like, 'When you're trying to pick up the path of the ball coming towards you, pick it up first as a line, then as a point.' I'd never really thought about things like that before," Ichiro recalled.

His coach's advice helped Ichiro become a player who relied not only on his skill but also on his power of thinking. That powerful combination—Ichiro the philosopher and the skilled batter—would make for a one-two punch as a player.

Chapter Five

One-Name Wonder

After the end of the 1993 season, Ichiro was sent to Hawaii to participate in a newly formed winter league. It was a chance for Ichiro to strut his stuff among Japanese players from other teams as well as Americans who were participating in the league. In this diverse environment, Ichiro thrived. Along with several other Blue Wave players, he was part of the Hilo Stars, and they helped the Stars win the league title.

It was a great time for Ichiro. He was playing every day, gaining confidence in himself, and was free to be himself and develop his style of play without being reprimanded for being different. As the league's season came to a close, Ichiro was one of the standout stars. He finished among the leaders in runs batted in (RBIs) and had a .311 batting average, fifth best in the league and more than 100 points higher than his average for the

Blue Wave in 1993. "In Hawaii, he showed he could hit as well as those big hitters who weren't from Japan," fellow Blue Wave outfielder So Taguchi recalled.

While in Hawaii, Ichiro received a piece of very surprising news. Although the Blue Wave had had a respectable 1993 season (they were three and a half games out of first place), the owners had fired manager Doi and hired Akira Ogi in his place. Ichiro felt that with a new manager, he could have a fresh start for the new season.

Ichiro first met Ogi in Hawaii, when he flew there to watch some of his new players in action. At first Ichiro was a little overwhelmed by Ogi's flashy appearance. He wore white shoes, white pants, a white belt, and gold sunglasses. Ichiro thought he looked like a Japanese gangster, or *yakuza.* Still, he was polite to his new manager. "I was bowled over. I was the youngest player, so I did my best to be courteous to him—pour drinks for him at meals and so on," Ichiro recalled.

❝ *Things were much more relaxed, the players were more lively; you knew if you gave it your all you'd get to play.* **❞**

—Ichiro on Akira Ogi taking over
the Orix Blue Wave in 1994

35

Ogi had been superstar pitcher Hideo Nomo's manager for three seasons when Nomo played for the Kintetsu Buffaloes. Ogi had a reputation for being a perfectionist but one who allowed his players to use their strengths without conforming to a regimented style. As long as his players gave their all and showed they were 100 percent behind the team, Ogi supported them.

With Ogi's support, Ichiro began hitting well in spring training. Freedom to be himself wasn't the only change for Ichiro. During 1994 spring training, Ogi suggested that Ichiro abandon "Suzuki," his last name, as the name on the back of his jersey. Instead he wanted "Ichiro" to appear as his official playing name. Ogi felt that changing his name to just "Ichiro" would bring him good luck in the coming season. He pointed out, "In professional baseball, there are eleven Suzukis, but there's only one Ichiro."

At first Ichiro thought Ogi was joking. When he realized he wasn't, he was worried. He didn't want people to think that he was conceited because he was referring to himself only by his first name. No player in Japanese baseball history had ever done that before. Ogi insisted that it was a good idea, so Ichiro agreed.

It took a little bit of getting used to. "I've got to admit," he said, "it embarrassed me when the public address announcers announced the starting lineup with me as 'Ichiro!,' not as 'Suzuki!,' and there was a great stir among the crowd."

"Ichiro Suzuki" is a very common name in Japan. It's the equivalent of "John Smith" in the United States.

But Ichiro quickly adjusted, and his playing began to reflect how comfortable he felt. At the beginning of the season, Ichiro set a goal to break a Japanese baseball record by making 200 hits (at that time, the record for a regular season was 191). Many thought it was an impossible feat, but Ichiro said, "I knew that I could reach my goal if I got at least five hits every three games."

Soon an energized Ichiro emerged. He was an unknown to most of the major-league pitchers, and he used that to his advantage. In his two years back and forth to the majors, he garnered a paltry .266 batting average. Since many of his major-league opponents were really only aware of his unimpressive major-league statistics (and hadn't paid attention to his notable minor-league stats), they didn't see him as a threat at the plate. But they were wrong.

In the first seventeen games of the 1994 season, Ichiro hit four home runs. His batting average was nearing .400. Ichiro became the talk of the nation. When he stepped up to the plate, the chants of "Ichiro! Ichiro!" could be heard throughout the stadium. Sportswriters were writing about him, and fans were talking about him. His baseball card was a coveted item to collect. It was very overwhelming to the young player.

> ❝ *There was a period when I felt the burden of everyone's expectations and I was chasing those stats.* ❞
>
> —Ichiro on trying to make the 200-hit mark in 1994

Ichiro, who was only twenty years old, kept his focus on hitting and with a cool head continued to make his ambition a reality. From May 21 to August 26, he had a continuous hitting streak of sixty-nine games before he was kept off base, a record for Japanese baseball. By mid-August the Blue Wave were holding on to first place in the Pacific League. Along with Ichiro, other key players included line-drive hitters Hirofumi Ogawa and Junichi Fukura. Pitchers Yoshinori Sato and Shigetoshi Hasegawa provided strong offense. Despite the strength of the team, in mid-September the Blue Wave's hopes to win the Pacific League pennant were dashed when they were swept in a four-game series by the Seibu Lions.

Although the Blue Wave had missed out on the league pennant, the regular season wasn't over. The day after the Blue Wave's disappointing loss to the Lions, Ichiro reached his goal and made Japanese sports history when he broke the 200-hit barrier. His batting average was also hovering at .400, another record (previously the highest batting average reached was .389). With Ichiro creating a sensation, attendance at Blue Wave games had improved by 4,000 fans per game.

In the end, Ichiro recorded an impressive .385 batting average for the season. "At that time I felt some power beyond just myself, sort of a divine force," he recalled. Ichiro's skills had been equally strong in the outfield. He was awarded a Gold Glove for his fielding abilities, and he was named the Pacific League's MVP (a rare honor for a player on a second-place team).

 Ichiro was the only member of the Orix Blue Wave to play in every one of his team's 130 games in 1994.

Suddenly the Japanese fans and media were debating whether Ichiro had the skill to handle American baseball pitches. Ichiro offered his own opinion. "As long as a ball is thrown by a human being, I have the confidence to hit any pitch, no matter how fast it comes," he said. He didn't want to seem arrogant, so he added, "I've never thought about playing in the [American] major leagues."

In reality, Ichiro wondered if he had what it would take to make it in the U.S. major leagues. In his third season with the Orix Blue Wave, Ichiro had come far. With his newfound fame came the realization that his life would never be the same again.

Chapter Six

Ichiromania

Ichiro fever had swept Japan and it showed no sign of slowing down. With his growing fame, Ichiro came to terms with the fact that he could no longer be anonymous. Everywhere he looked, some sort of paraphernalia was devoted to him—photos, buttons, jewelry, banners, and trading cards.

In the 1994 season, Ichiro had been riding to the ballpark with teammate So Taguchi but decided to buy his own car in 1995 so that he could get some much-needed privacy. Unlike other players, who would allow reporters to huddle around their cars after a game, Ichiro asked the press to keep their distance from his car. Although they respected his wishes, they didn't stop speaking to him whenever they could. It was the beginning of Ichiro's sometimes difficult relationship with the press.

"I'd always kept in the background up till then, so I was overwhelmed as one [reporter] after another came after me,"

Ichiro commented. "I was happy about it, but the truth was it was a little scary with all kinds of people popping up. After the '94 season ended I couldn't go out for a stroll anytime I wanted like before."

And then Ichiro's mind became focused on something much more serious. On January 17, 1995, a colossal earthquake (7.2 on the Richter scale) hit the city of Kobe, the Blue Wave's hometown, and killed more than 6,000 people. Ichiro was in the team's dormitory when the natural disaster hit. "I can't put into words how frightening it was. My room was on the fourth floor of the dorm, and I was afraid the floor was going to give out. My stereo speakers and TV toppled over. Fortunately, the only damage was some cracks in the wall of the dorm, but the town of Kobe . . . was destroyed," he said.

When the disaster happened, a shaken Ichiro packed some of his things and decided to do his off-season training at his home near Nagoya. The rumor mill began churning that Ichiro had deserted Kobe in its time of need. That wasn't the case. Ichiro had just gone home to center himself after the terrible tragedy, but being a high-profile personality made him a target for such speculation.

Ichiro's honest desire to help Kobe get back on its feet soon became evident. The city began a campaign called the "Kobe Comeback," and at the center of it were Ichiro and his Blue

Wave teammates, who wanted to do whatever they could to boost the morale of their city.

At the start of the 1995 season, all of the Blue Wave players had their uniforms decorated with sleeve patches that read *Gambarou Kobe,* which means "Let's Do Our Best for Kobe!" Ichiro was touched that despite all the hardship Kobe's residents had gone through, fans still showed up to see their hometown team play. "They'd gone through much and you'd think baseball wasn't much of a priority, but they still came to cheer us on. That encouraged us a lot, and we did our best to live up to their expectations," Ichiro recalled.

The Blue Wave were determined to reach the Japan Series for their beleaguered town. One of the toughest obstacles on their quest was the Chiba Lotte Marines. Pitcher Hideki Irabu was a formidable opponent for Ichiro. Their showdowns during the 1995 season became legendary. Every time Ichiro would get up to bat against Irabu, he knew that he would have his work cut out for him. Rather than intimidate Ichiro, though, Irabu's power brought out the best in him.

"In the whole stadium you could tell that something was different between the two of us," Ichiro recalled. "Which is why it was so interesting when we faced off against each other. Even when he got me out I still felt good about that at bat."

Feeding off Irabu's energy made Ichiro that much more

excited about making the season a winning one. The only difficult thing for Ichiro was that the Blue Wave management had switched his order in the batting roster, from the leadoff spot to third.

Ichiro had been an ideal leadoff batter. The leadoff batter hits for a high on-base average and gets on base by any means possible—grounders, pop flys, bunts, walks, and so on. In Ichiro's case, he also made pitchers work very hard throwing pitches, which can really tire them out. He was known for high scoring and for his speed getting to base. The third batter has a different set of skills. He's normally the best hitter on the team (think Barry Bonds). He's the guy who can come through with a clutch hit and drive in runs. Ichiro later said, "It was very tough to bat third. Batting leadoff was the perfect spot for me. I could totally focus on hitting when I was first. It feels great to be the leadoff batter and get a hit. Batting third, it's a completely different feeling you get standing there in the batter's box."

Ichiro was such a strong all-around hitter that the Blue Wave felt he would do well in either spot. But mentally Ichiro had a hard time adjusting to the switch. "My batting average had gone way down . . . and I was really doing poorly," he commented. Realizing what the problem was, the team moved him back to the top spot on the batting roster.

As the 1995 season came to a close, the Blue Wave lost their last four home games. "I felt terrible when we couldn't clinch it at home in Kobe," Ichiro said. "Nobody booed us or anything, but you could hear this huge sigh come up from the whole stadium. It was really tough to see how discouraged the fans were."

The Blue Wave rebounded as they headed on the road, beating the Seibu Lions and finishing as the Pacific League champions. Ichiro had something extra to cheer him up. He was awarded the league's batting title and was named MVP for the second year in a row. The star topped the Pacific League in hits, runs, RBIs, stolen bases, on-base percentage, and total bases. In addition, Ichiro had hit twenty-five home runs. He was a source of pride for Kobe.

With the league championship neatly tied up, the Blue Wave headed to the 1995 Japan Series, where they faced the Yakult Swallows. Unfortunately, the Swallows won the first three games in the best-of-seven series. The hitting of Central League MVP Tom O'Malley and the pitching of Terry Bross gave Ichiro and his teammates a hard time. Although the Blue Wave scored a win in game four, the next day the Swallows took home the victory. The Swallows had done everything in their power to make sure Ichiro didn't get on base—including trying to attack him with inside pitches. "When we lost the series 1–4 it was such a shock that all those happy feelings we had winning the pennant just flew out the window," Ichiro admitted.

But Ichiro was ready for a fresh start when the 1996 season began. The Blue Wave team was strong, and with Ichiro at its center, they felt confident that they could make it to the Japan Series and win.

Ichiro's popularity was at an all-time high. In fact, a minor crime spree was committed because of him. When the slugger began sporting a pair of yellow Nike Air Max sneakers, the demand for the shoes became so high that a gang of robbers attacked several teenagers in Osaka by shoe jacking (called *oi hagi*) them right off their feet!

As the season progressed, Ichiro just kept getting hotter. By June he was leading the Pacific League with a .324 batting average. In August, Ichiro marked his twenty-second game in a row with more than three base hits per game, showing his skill as a precise batter. The record of twenty-one games had previously been held by sluggers Wally Yonamine and Isao Harimoto. With a .359 batting average in August, Ichiro just couldn't seem to miss!

Even though the Blue Wave trailed Tokyo's Nippon Ham Fighters for much of the season, Orix eventually came out on top. Ichiro won another batting crown with a .356 average. He also drove in 193 hits and 104 runs and won the MVP award for the third year in a row. It was clear to fans that Ichiro was a player with staying power.

After winning the Pacific League championship, the Blue Wave still had a tough battle ahead of them. They had to face the Yomiuri Giants in the Japan Series. The Yomiuri Giants in Japan are much like the New York Yankees in the United States—the top team to beat. "It's a completely different atmosphere when you're playing the Giants. It's like there's an authority that comes with them," Ichiro explained.

The country couldn't wait for the matchup. Tickets for the series went on sale on October 11, 1996, and 29,000 people lined up in front of the Tokyo Dome to buy them.

On October 19, the series got off to an exciting start. In the first game, Ichiro knocked in a home run against Giants pitcher Hirofumi Kono in the tenth inning, helping his team win the game. Interestingly, Ichiro said that he had not intended to hit a home run. "I was positive the next pitch would be outside. I had this mental image of this straight, outside ball, but the second it left the pitcher's hands I saw it coming high and down the middle. I made an instantaneous adjustment."

That win set the stage for a series of wins for the Blue Wave. The next day, the Blue Wave trounced the Giants, 2–0. All the while, Ichiro was a ball of energy in the outfield, hearing happy screams every time he fielded a ball and made a play. By the end of the series, which the Blue Wave won, 4–1, Ichiro had reached base seven times. He was an integral factor in the Blue

Wave winning their first Japan Series championship since moving to Kobe in 1989.

❝People said, 'Now that you're the best in Japan you can't top that, can you?' but that's not true.❞
—ICHIRO ON WINNING THE 1996 JAPAN SERIES

In fact, Ichiro felt that being the underdogs in the series was an advantage for the Blue Wave because no one really expected them to win against the Giants. But the Blue Wave would no longer have the underdog status on their side. Ichiro had made a name for himself as a batter to be reckoned with across both the Pacific and the Central Leagues.

After the 1996 season, Ichiro joined the Japanese All-Star squad, which played a series of games against top American players like Pedro Martinez, Cal Ripken Jr., Barry Bonds, and Mike Piazza. The U.S.–Japan All-Star series takes place every other year, and it is always played in Japan. Because of the 1994 U.S. baseball players' strike, the series had not been played since 1992. Ichiro was elated to be on the team, and he was determined to make the most of his opportunity.

In his first game, Ichiro batted against pitchers Pat Hentgen and Pedro Martinez and went two for three (two hits in three at bats) with two walks. During the series, Ichiro went head-to-head with former Japanese star Hideo Nomo, who had become a top pitcher with the Los Angeles Dodgers. In his first at bat against Nomo, Ichiro succeeded in rapping out a single.

Ichiro impressed the American All-Stars with his hitting, stealing, and fielding abilities. And Ichiro was impressed with the Americans' fearlessness when it came to hitting. They'd slam out homers with no worry that they'd be reprimanded for showboating. It was a new concept for Ichiro and one that he embraced.

---

66 *[Ichiro is] one of the top five players in the world. He's the real thing.* 99

—BOBBY VALENTINE, FORMER CHIBA LOTTE MARINES MANAGER AND EX–NEW YORK METS MANAGER

Ultimately the U.S. squad walked away victorious. They had four wins, two losses, and two ties. Ichiro had seven hits in his eleven series at bats, proving that he could handle the heat the U.S. players were throwing his way. Mike Piazza, star slugger for the New York Mets, even commented to the Japanese press that he thought Ichiro had the skills to succeed in the U.S. major leagues. Ichiro's response to the compliment was coy. "I could go, but I would be the batboy," he joked.

One of the constraints Ichiro faced was his contract with the Blue Wave. Like all Japanese baseball players, he was obligated to spend nine years playing in the major leagues with his team (minor-league play doesn't count) before he would be a free agent. Only free agents are allowed to choose to join other teams in Japan or abroad. Despite the rules, a desire had been sparked in Ichiro. "I saw these good American players," he said, "and I wanted to play against them."

Chapter | Seven

Time for Change

The start of the 1997 season wasn't easy for Ichiro. Playing with the American All-Stars had been exciting. Yet once that series was over, Ichiro felt like it was back to business as usual with the Blue Wave.

The season did not get off to a strong start for the team. "It was pretty lame," recalled Ichiro. "In that atmosphere, a batter has to work to get results since raising your spirits and maintaining your motivation is definitely difficult." Ichiro began struggling with his own batting form. "Every single day was a struggle for me because I just wasn't hitting the way I wanted to," he revealed.

Another challenge was the level of scrutiny Ichiro was undergoing because of his popularity. Ichiro topped the list of Japanese celebrities. Everywhere he went, people were clamoring for his autograph.

In 1997 Ichiro started selling his own clothing line in Japan. Within weeks it was the top-selling brand in the country.

Despite all the distractions off the field, while he was playing, Ichiro exhibited the focus and clarity for which he was famous. Between April 16 and June 25 of the 1997 season, Ichiro made a record 216 consecutive plate appearances without striking out.

Throughout the season, Ichiro had wowed the stadiums with his crowd-pleasing ways. Everything about his performance during a game was magnetic. Fans liked the way he held his bat, cocking it toward the pitcher as if he was about to have a duel and then sweeping it into a hitting position. He also played catch with the spectators during warm-ups. He even snuck onto the pitcher's mound and threw the ball to the catcher, as if he was going to pitch the game. The crowds loved it all.

At moments like these, the twenty-four-year-old Ichiro was able to show his childlike love for the game. Yet when it came time to be serious, Ichiro was all business. He knew that he had become a role model to kids across the nation. It was a position he took very seriously. "Once I put on that [number] 51 I feel I'm Ichiro, the professional ballplayer, and that's how I act," he explained.

Ichiro capped off the season by winning his fourth-straight batting title with a .345 average. He also knocked in a career-best ninety-one runs. These accomplishments still weren't enough to snag the Pacific League MVP award. That honor went to pitcher Fumiya Nishiguchi of the Seibu Lions.

Despite constantly being in the spotlight during the season, the eligible young bachelor found someone special in his private life. He began dating sportscaster Yumiko Fukushima in the fall of 1997. As a baseball superstar, Ichiro couldn't conduct a normal courtship. He couldn't just pick up Yumiko and go to a restaurant or to the movies. They had to be secretive about their every move so that they wouldn't be tailed by photographers and reporters.

Ichiro once evaded the press by having his friends roll him up in a carpet and take him in a pickup truck to meet Yumiko! Another night, when Ichiro and Yumiko decided to go for a romantic drive to Mount Rokko in Kobe, so many people had gone up there that they couldn't even get out of the car to enjoy the view.

The outfielder also began to resent that he wasn't always portrayed accurately to the public. "If the person who reads one of those untrue articles is a friend of mine I can give him the real story, but some people don't get the Pacific League games on TV, or live near a ballpark, and all they know about Ichiro the player is what they read in those articles," he explained.

When the 1998 season rolled around, the Blue Wave were still suffering from low morale. Two of their key American players, including home run hitter Troy Neel, had headed back to the United States, and the Blue Wave pitching staff wasn't doing well. The whole team seemed to be in a slump.

Ichiro tried hard to stay centered, and he kept his concentration on his batting and fielding. In 1998 he earned a .358 batting average, scored the league's most base hits (181), and won his fifth Gold Glove award. But he stole only eleven bases during the entire season (down from thirty-nine the previous year). Close observers of the game interpreted the low number of stolen bases as a sign that Ichiro was finding it hard to keep up his enthusiasm. "I didn't lose my desire to play in Japan, but it wasn't interesting to me anymore," he later confessed.

Although things were tough with his team, Ichiro's personal life continued to go well. He and Yumiko got engaged in the fall of 1998. "I could be myself with her, completely. And she said the same thing. Another big factor was that she got along really well with my parents," he revealed.

Ichiro was also excited about participating in another

postseason series against the Americans in the dual-country All-Star series in early November. The eight-game exhibition took place in Tokyo, Fukuoka, and Osaka. Once again the Americans won the series, 6–2. Even though the Japan team lost more games than they won, Ichiro impressed the Americans with his playing. Against the likes of Sammy Sosa, Curt Schilling, and Nomar Garciaparra, he performed with force and grace.

He was a key player in both games won by the Japanese. In one he got three hits in five at bats, with two stolen bases. In another Ichiro drove in the only run in a 1–0 Japanese victory. After experiencing Ichiro's power on the field, Cleveland Indians manager Mike Hargrove, who managed the American All-Stars, told the Japanese press, "Before I got here, I hadn't heard of Ichiro, but I am very impressed. He has above-average ability in hitting and throwing." Seattle Mariners pitcher Jamie Moyer had even higher praise, raving, "[Ichiro] has a great batting eye, and I'm not sure I've seen anyone in the majors quicker from home to first base than him."

After the All-Star game, the Blue Wave management sensed that Ichiro needed a change of pace. They decided to send him—along with two Blue Wavers, pitchers Nobuyuki Hoshino and Nobuyuki Ebisu—to attend two weeks of spring training with the Seattle Mariners. They would also have the chance to play in the first four games of the exhibition season. Ichiro was excited to make another trip to the United States, his first since going to Hawaii in 1993. Moreover, he was going to be playing side by side with Ken Griffey Jr., whose talent he had long admired.

At the end of February, Ichiro arrived at the Mariners' spring training camp in Peoria, Arizona. It was a new world for Ichiro, who spoke to his "teammates" through a translator. He asked their advice about playing, joked around, picked up English slang like "wassup?" and had the time of his life. He felt rejuvenated among the U.S. players and happy to be in a new environment. His playing reflected his enthusiasm. He was supercharged and hitting and fielding in top form. "That was an exciting time for me," Ichiro later said.

Mariners manager Lou Piniella was equally impressed with Ichiro, saying, "He had a flair to him. He carried himself like a superstar player."

Ichiro tried to take in whatever information he could, and Moyer, who had admired Ichiro's playing in Japan, said that Ichiro's "biggest question [was] always, 'Can I play in the U.S.?'" He was a question machine, querying the players on what it was like to face all the different pitchers in the league, trying to get a sense of their hitting strategies and, most importantly, what it would take for him to be successful in the U.S. major leagues.

Another huge benefit of being in a new country was that he wasn't famous and was treated just like the other players. He was just Ichiro, baseball player, not Ichiro, superstar. He didn't have the press following him everywhere he went, and he could actually shop and eat out at restaurants without being mobbed by fans. He had forgotten what that kind of freedom felt like!

The weeks in Peoria taught Ichiro a lot. More and more, Ichiro realized that he needed a change and that playing in America could provide that for him. The Mariners were open about admitting that Ichiro had the stuff to be an integral part of their team. Roger Jongewaard, the team's vice president for scouting, said at the time, "He could be a leadoff hitter or a number two hitter and get a couple of hundred hits for us. He'd be perfect in our lineup."

But the Mariners had to make it clear that they weren't trying to steal the Blue Wave's star player. Ichiro wouldn't be eligible until 2001 to try his hand at becoming a U.S. major leaguer. The Mariners wanted to ensure that they would continue to have good relations with the Blue Wave in the years to come.

Unfortunately, Ichiro suffered a bad case of food poisoning and couldn't play in the Mariners' final two exhibition games. But his illness didn't stop him from feeling reinvigorated. The minute he began fielding and hitting with his American counterparts, he'd reignited his spark. In addition, his time in America only strengthened his conviction that one day he'd make his mark in the U.S. major leagues.

    ❝*If anybody in Japan could come over and have success, it's Ichiro, because he's so fundamentally sound in everything he does.***❞**
—FORMER SEATTLE MARINERS BATTING COACH JESSE BARFIELD

Ichiro hurls his best pitch during the Koshien high school baseball tournament.

While he played for the Orix Blue Wave, Ichiro amazed other teams with his blistering baserunning. Here, in 2000, he dashes to first base during a game against the Nippon Ham Fighters in the Tokyo Dome.

In November of 2000, Ichiro signed a three-year contract with the Seattle Mariners. Following the signing, the Mariners held a press conference at which Ichiro tried on his new jersey and posed with Mariners CEO Howard Lincoln.

Before each at bat, Ichiro goes through a regimented series of stretches to make sure that he's in top condition.

Ichiro shows total focus as he faces the New York Yankees at Yankee Stadium. The Mariners won 9–5.

As an outfielder, Ichiro wowed Mariners fans with his awesome throwing ability. In this June 2001 game, the Mariners beat the Anaheim Angels 5–3.

Ichiro's fans showed their support in English and in Japanese at this 2001 game against the Colorado Rockies. The Japanese signs show Ichiro's name, spelled in katakana characters.

Ichiro shows off his second straight Gold Glove award, given for his accomplishments in the outfield in 2002. He received the award before an April 2003 game against the Anaheim Angels. The Mariners won 5–0.

Ichiro wears sunglasses to protect his eyes, but they have also become part of his trademark style, popular on both sides of the Pacific Ocean.

Chapter | Eight

Dream Come True

Ichiro came back to Japan from Arizona feeling changed. He had lived his U.S. major-league dreams, however briefly. He also got to witness the way players in America expressed themselves. And he noticed that the "looser" the players were, the better their performance was. That was a new notion for him because he was used to the rigidity and seriousness of Japanese baseball coaches. "Everybody in the States is so relaxed," he said at the time, "and everybody in Japan is so uptight."

When he returned, Ichiro looked and seemed different. He had grown a funky goatee, which gave him a distinctly different appearance than many of the clean-cut players in the Japanese leagues. He had also embraced aspects of American culture, dressing in baggy clothes and listening to hip-hop music.

Ichiro wasn't in Japan very long before he was back in the news. In his seventh season with Orix, Ichiro signed the most lucrative contract in the history of Japanese baseball, a one-year contract worth 500 million yen (approximately $4.15 million). Although that amount might have seemed small to some U.S. baseball players, it was a huge sum for a Japanese ballplayer to earn. The Blue Wave were clearly trying to show Ichiro how much they believed in him. They also worried that Ichiro wanted to jump ship to join the U.S. majors, and they wanted to do everything in their power to keep their star hitter happy.

Ichiro should've been ecstatic about his new contract, but he had more pressing concerns. He wanted to get to the bottom of something that had been bothering him for several seasons. Although no one could have sensed there was anything wrong since he was hitting so well, Ichiro felt that a subtle batting problem had been holding him back from realizing his full potential.

"The four years '95 to '98, it was a constant struggle to get to the top," he explained. "I don't think many people were aware of this, though. People kept praising me, saying how great my batting was . . . but those numbers hid the deep despair I was secretly feeling over my batting. . . . I often felt lost and, deep down, never really believed in my abilities as a ballplayer."

In the beginning of the 1999 season, Ichiro faced a batting slump in which he just couldn't seem to get a hit. "When I went after a pitch, just before I hit it I couldn't follow it with my eyes.

Batters don't just hit with their bodies, but you zero in on the ball coming toward you with your eyes and the information you pick up visually is what you use to make contact with your bat. . . . And that's what I couldn't do at the time," he revealed.

On April 11, 1999, Ichiro and the Blue Wave were playing against the Seibu Lions at the Nagoya Dome. It was the last game of a three-game series. In the ninth inning, Ichiro was the leadoff batter against Lions pitcher Yukihiro Nishizaki. Up until that point in the game, Ichiro had hit into easy outs three of the four times he was at bat. He hit a weak grounder to second and was thrown out at first base. The hit was far from spectacular, but it caused a lightbulb to go off in Ichiro's head. As he was running to first base, he connected the mental image of his batting form with the form he had when he grounded out to second base. "The timing and the swing I'd been searching for I found in that instant. This wasn't some vague image, but something I could grasp totally with my mind and body," he recalled.

Ichiro headed back to the dugout with a huge smile on his face. Of course, his manager was not pleased to see him grinning after getting yet another out. He had no way to know that Ichiro had just discovered the source of his problem. For several years, the angle of his front right foot had been off slightly when he was batting and caused the angle with which he stepped into pitches to be off-kilter. It was interfering with his timing.

It was such a tiny difference (literally a matter of a few millimeters), but it was enough of a margin of error to throw Ichiro off his game, making getting precise hits that much harder. "If that angle is off, then even if you think you're able to get to the ball perfectly, you'll end up hitting into an easy out," he later explained. "Thanks to that seemingly meaningless ground out to the second baseman, the internal sensor I needed was somehow magically activated. . . . It's possible I could have gone through my entire career fruitlessly searching for that feeling without ever having found it."

His discovery was a turning point for Ichiro, who felt like a changed man. He sensed that he could get on with the game at hand without any more doubts about his batting clouding his mind. In late April, he notched his 1,000th career hit. He made his mark with a bang—it was a home run! By reaching 1,000 hits in 757 games, he set a new Japanese baseball record. As the season progressed, Ichiro emerged as a new player. On July 6, in a game against the Seibu Lions, Ichiro swatted his 100th career home run off pitcher Daisuke Matsuzaka.

Just when everything was going so well, on August 24, in a game against the Nippon Ham Fighters—Ichiro's 763rd consecutive game in the major leagues—Ichiro was hit by a pitch. He'd stood farther back in the batter's box than he usually did, and the pitcher hit him with a screwball. Ichiro winced in pain as the ball made contact with his wrist. Immediately he knew it wasn't a normal injury. "It felt really bad 'cause it hit the part underneath the wrist where there's hardly any flesh," he recalled. "There was this immediate flash of pain." Ichiro was diagnosed with a broken wrist and had to undergo rehabilitation, forcing him to miss the final five weeks of the season. He finished out the 1999 season with a .343 batting average.

Being away from the field gave Ichiro something he hadn't had in a long while: free time. He did things he normally couldn't, like going to concerts and eating out with friends. "It was a positive thing for me to be able to see a different world for a while, for a change of pace," he said.

Ichiro also continued doing some serious soul-searching. Ever since he had returned from Arizona, he felt more and more the desire to go to America and become a major leaguer there. Previously, wanting to go to the United States was an effort to escape his batting problem. After coming to terms with it, he had a different motivation. He simply wanted to play the game at the highest level possible, and Ichiro felt that place was the United States.

Of course, the fact that Ichiro couldn't go until his contract expired in 2001 remained a barrier. He tried to talk to the Blue Wave management about his desire to go, but his request was refused. When his mentor and manager, Akira Ogi, asked him to let the matter rest and not pursue it, Ichiro agreed. Ogi had done so much for him and his career, Ichiro didn't want to upset or disappoint him.

By 1999 Ichiro's popularity had reached such an intense level that mail simply addressed to "Ichiro/Japan" would get delivered to him!

Ichiro decided to put his move to the U.S. majors on the back burner—for the moment—and focus his energy on getting back into shape for the 2000 season. He and Yumiko were also secretly planning their wedding. Because of Ichiro's popularity and the press's thirst to know everything about him, the couple had to keep their nuptial plans under wraps. "Marriage was such an important decision in our lives that we really wanted to be able to approach it as a shared personal event, the way we feel is appropriate, without any kind of media frenzy."

Ichiro and Yumiko decided that getting married anywhere in Japan would be too risky. Instead they opted to have their wedding at the Riviera Country Club in Los Angeles. Their parents were disappointed that their children wouldn't be having a large reception but soon agreed that keeping it small and private was the best idea. Ichiro and Yumiko's friends helped a great deal with the wedding planning. They helped get Ichiro's tuxedo made, bought the rings, and flew ahead to Los Angeles to decorate the country club for the ceremony and reception.

To avoid giving any hints about what they were planning, Ichiro and Yumiko traveled on separate flights to Los Angeles. When the big day, December 3, 1999, finally arrived, Ichiro was very excited. Dressed in a beige tuxedo, he stood by an arch made of roses and watched as his bride, wearing a simple dress she had bought on a trip to Spain, walked down the aisle escorted by her father. In attendance were both their families and four or five friends. After exchanging vows in English, Ichiro kissed his bride. It was a blissful moment.

Following an intimate dinner at the country club's restaurant, Ichiro reflected on the wonderful day—and how grateful he was to his friends for helping him pull it off! "I broke down and cried. Everybody looked at me like they couldn't figure out why, of all times, I'm crying now," he later confessed with a laugh. "Without all of them we never would have gotten married. . . . After it was all over I thought to myself, 'What a wonderful thing a wedding is.'"

Ichiro didn't have long to bask in his newfound joy. Before long, he was heading to spring training at Miyakojima, a southern Japanese island. To make sure he was fully recovered from his injury, Ichiro hadn't played baseball from August until January. He had the difficult task of getting his stiff arm back into shape but didn't want to overdo it. "I did all my training at my own pace," he recalled. After several days of training, Ichiro felt his batting was back on course.

In Japan, unlike in the United States, professional baseball players commonly clean their own gloves and shoes.

Ichiro knew it was only a matter of time before he again mentioned the subject of leaving the Blue Wave for the United States, but he wasn't about to let his team down for the new season. In fact, he set a goal for himself to end the season with a .400 batting average. "Finally, I felt everything I needed to achieve that level was in place. I felt that if I was able to make contact with 60 to 70 percent of the strikes thrown to me, hitting .400 wasn't out of the realm of possibility."

As the season progressed, Ichiro bounced between a solid .350 and .400 average. On August 26, when Ichiro had returned from a road trip with the team, he could feel a tenderness in his right side. Not thinking it was anything serious, he decided to go for a jog. Unfortunately, it aggravated the pain.

The next day, when Ichiro got up to bat in the bottom of the third inning in a game against the Chiba Lotte Marines, he fouled off a slider. At the moment of impact, he knew something was wrong. He didn't want to stop playing, though, so he headed to his spot in the outfield in the fourth inning. After catching a fly ball, he attempted to throw it and discovered that he couldn't raise his arm above shoulder level. He was taken out of the game and sent to the hospital. There they diagnosed him with an inflammation of the muscles. Ichiro was told he would have to sit out the rest of the season.

Even though he hadn't reached his goal, Ichiro finished the year 2000 with a stellar .387 average. Ichiro used his recovery period as an opportunity to talk to those he trusted about his desire to go to the United States. One night Ogi invited Ichiro and Yumiko to dinner. During their discussion, he told Ichiro that he wouldn't oppose his decision to leave. Ichiro was happy to have his blessing, but he still had to get approval from the Blue Wave's president.

Reluctantly the Blue Wave agreed to give Ichiro the option, and on October 12, 2000, Ichiro announced that he wanted to use the posting system to switch over to the American majors. The posting system is an agreement between U.S. Major League Baseball (MLB) and the Japanese leagues that was established after Hideki Irabu was signed to the Yankees in 1997. It allows a baseball club to in essence put a player on the international market and auction him to the highest bidder. Some players don't like the system because it doesn't allow them to decide which team to join. Only after serving in the Japanese majors for nine years is a player allowed to make the choice.

"For a number of years I have had the feeling that I would like to take a shot at playing in the majors," Ichiro said in a press conference about being allowed the option to be posted. "I'm happy I've reached an agreement with the club to open up this possibility."

The next day was bittersweet. Ichiro attended his final game as a member of the Orix Blue Wave. A packed crowd turned up to bid farewell to their beloved baseball star. He was still too sore from his injury to hit, but in the ninth inning he came into the game for his final appearance as an outfielder. Ichiro got a standing ovation.

❝*I want to be the first player to show what Japanese batters can do in the major leagues.***❞**

—ICHIRO

On November 1, the Blue Wave officially made Ichiro available to the MLB bidders. Ichiro had made it obvious that this was what he wanted, and the last thing the team wanted was an unhappy player. Of course, it wouldn't hurt that the Blue Wave would earn a hefty sum of money in exchange for trading him.

After the Blue Wave "posted" Ichiro, it was up to American teams to show their interest. The Seattle Mariners, the New York Mets, the Los Angeles Dodgers, the Anaheim Angels, and several other teams all placed bids. Posting bids happens in secret, and on November 9, the highest bidder was announced. The Mariners were the victorious team. They agreed to pay $13.1 million to the Blue Wave outright and more than $15 million to Ichiro over a three-year period. The contract also included English lessons for Ichiro and Yumiko, a personal trainer, an interpreter, an annual housing allowance, four round-trip plane tickets from Japan to Seattle, and the use of a car. Not a bad deal!

Ichiro was thrilled to join Seattle's team as a right fielder. He had thoroughly enjoyed his time with the Mariners during spring training in 1999. He also loved the idea of living in Seattle, which boasts a large Japanese American population. Plus his pal relief pitcher Kazuhiro Sasaki was on the team. "Being able to play for Seattle is the realization of a dream," he said after getting the news. Ichiro was ready for the next phase of his life.

Chapter Nine

Making Waves

To officially announce Ichiro's trade, the Seattle Mariners asked Ichiro and Yumiko to attend a press conference at the team's Safeco Field on November 30. Ichiro had to practically pinch himself. He had spent years longing for this moment, and it was finally here!

The local press were surprised to see more than fifty Japanese reporters at the press conference. They hadn't known just how much of a celebrity Ichiro was in his homeland. They also got a sense of Ichiro's popularity when a group of visiting Japanese schoolgirls caught a glimpse of their icon and began screaming.

After returning to Japan and saying good-bye to their family and friends, Ichiro and Yumiko packed up their belongings and made the big move to Seattle. The best part of adjusting to life in the United States for Ichiro was that at least temporarily, he had his freedom back. "I really enjoy being able to go anywhere without people noticing me," Ichiro said at the time. Yumiko, he said, "is even happier than I am."

Ichiro and Yumiko enlisted the help of the Mariners to find a three-bedroom apartment. Ichiro wanted extra room so that he could have a space just to practice his swings inside his home. That's dedication!

After finding a new home, it wasn't long before Ichiro had to report to spring training in Peoria, Arizona. Ichiro's arrival followed the off-season departure of famed shortstop Alex Rodriguez. In recent years, the team had also traded away slugger Ken Griffey Jr. and pitcher Randy Johnson. Mariners fans hoped that Ichiro's skill could help fill the void on the team.

Ichiro got to spring training ahead of most of the Mariners, and he was understandably nervous. He was greeted by a throng of nearly 150 Japanese reporters who had flown to Arizona to report on his every move. They recorded how many swings he took, how he warmed up, and how he was holding his bat. Ichiro was understandably irritated. "I didn't expect them to watch every move I make, from the time I get to the parking lot to the time I leave the parking lot. It's unnecessary. How many times do they have to see me stretch? How many times do they have to see me walk?" he said, exasperated.

The Japanese reporters were in for a rude surprise when they found out that the Mariners had set up special rules for them to follow. The Mariners told them that they would have to submit their questions to one Japanese reporter, Keizo Konishi of the Kyodo News Service, who would then convey them to Ichiro. Ichiro would answer the question Konishi asked, but he would not speak with any of the other reporters. The Japanese press sent to America to cover Ichiro's comings and goings were crestfallen. But they were willing to take whatever they could get.

❝ *I would not wish to say without first asking its permission.* **❞**

—ICHIRO'S RESPONSE TO A REPORTER'S QUESTION
ABOUT HIS DOG'S NAME

Ichiro, meanwhile, got down to the business at hand of meeting all the coaches and players. To help prepare him for all the new pitchers he'd be facing in the coming season, ever-diligent Ichiro asked to have a video made showing all the teams in the order that they'd be playing them. He studied the tapes carefully.

Ichiro was happy to find out that the Mariners had agreed to let him keep his first name on his jersey and the number 51. That made him feel more at home, even though it caused some controversy among longtime fans. Star Mariner pitcher Randy Johnson had been number 51 until he was traded to Houston in 1998, and some felt that his number should have been retired. The fans weren't sure whether their new player would live up to the history behind the number. Ichiro reacted by sending a personal message to Johnson, promising, "I won't bring shame to the number."

As Ichiro settled in to spring training, he began showing off the skills that had made the Mariners eager to sign him. He wowed his teammates with his incredible speed (clocking in at 3.7 seconds to first base!), his throwing arm, and his skill as an outfielder. Still, they were curious to see how he would hit.

Before a game, Ichiro always massages a six-inch wooden stick up and down the bottoms of his feet. "It's for pressure points," he explained.

The Mariners' first game of the exhibition season was a charity event against the San Diego Padres, and it was televised live in Japan at 5:00 AM. In his first appearance, Ichiro didn't make a great showing. "Pitchers are knocking bats out of his hands," one scout scoffed. As Ichiro kept hitting grounders, Mariners manager Lou Piniella began getting nervous. He wondered if Ichiro would be able to handle the U.S. major-league pitchers.

When Piniella expressed his concern directly to Ichiro, he told Piniella not to worry. Ichiro let him in on a secret—he knew exactly what he was doing. "I'm just setting them up," Ichiro confided, referring to the pitchers he was playing against. Just as he'd done at the beginning of his major-league career in Japan, Ichiro wanted to use the fact that they didn't know what he was capable of against them. Fellow outfielder Al Martin was skeptical, saying, "Nobody is that good. You don't just walk into your first spring training, hang around, and set people up."

 Ichiro's not only a baseball star, he's also a fan. He loves to get autographs from other baseball players.

Soon Piniella and Martin had every reason to have confidence in the new player. A few days after Piniella and Ichiro had their talk, Ichiro began hitting line drives in the exhibition games and even knocked in a home run.

Ichiro was also fitting in with his teammates. Although he had to communicate through an interpreter, they soon got to see glimpses of his personality. He did imitations of sportscasters and rapped Snoop Dogg lyrics. He formed a fast friendship with center fielder Mike Cameron. He also impressed his teammates with his knowledge of American baseball history and his excitement about visiting famous ballparks like New York's Yankee Stadium and Boston's Fenway Park.

At the start of the official season, Piniella had thought about putting Ichiro third in the batting order, then he changed his mind and left him in the leadoff position. After Ichiro's performance at the opening day game on April 2, 2001 against the Oakland A's, Piniella knew that he had made the right decision.

On April 6, in the eleventh inning of an extra-long game in Texas against the Rangers, Ichiro hit his first U.S. major-league home run. Ichiro laughed when recalling the reaction from his teammates. "I think everybody thought it was just a fluke. That had to be what they were thinking, the way they carried on when I hit it."

They'd soon see that Ichiro was capable of a lot. On April 11, Ichiro and the Mariners were playing the A's, this time in Oakland. Ichiro wasn't in the starting lineup because Piniella wanted to give him a rest so that he could remain in top shape for the season. In the still-scoreless eighth inning, Piniella changed his mind and realized he could use a dose of Ichiro power.

Ichiro stepped up to the plate and hit a single into left field to bring in the first run of the game. In the bottom of the inning, Ichiro—now officially in the game—was stationed in right field. A's outfielder Terrence Long came up to bat. He singled down the middle. Following him to the plate was pinch hitter Ramon Hernandez. Ichiro got ready for anything that might happen next. If Hernandez hit the ball into the gap between right and center field, he'd have to be quick on his feet to retrieve it. If he hit a fly ball, Ichiro would have to make a clean catch and then rocket it to second base so that Long couldn't advance.

Hernandez slugged the ball to right field, where it hit the ground to become a base hit. Ichiro sprang into action. He saw Long round second and head for third base. Ichiro caught the ball on a hop while running at full speed. In one motion, Ichiro rocketed the ball all the way from right field smack-dab to third baseman David Bell, who tagged out Long. Ichiro had made the perfect throw.

For a moment, the umpire wasn't sure if Bell really had the ball. When he determined that Ichiro had actually made that incredible launch, he screamed, "Out!" A standing ovation erupted in the stands. The Mariners won the game, 3–0.

The press went wild, trying to drum up ways to describe the throw that Ichiro had made. One reporter for the *Seattle Times* called it a "200-foot lightning bolt that was never more than a few feet off the ground." Another writer, for the *Seattle Post-Intelligencer,* said that Ichiro's throw "needs to be framed and hung on the wall at the Louvre, next to the *Mona Lisa.* It was that much a thing of beauty."

Ichiro had a lot of surprises in store. In a game a few days later, Ichiro intercepted what would have been a home run by the Texas Rangers' Rafael Palmeiro. And his impressive plays just kept on coming. He was rapidly winning the loyalty of

Mariners fans, who began chanting, "Ichiro! Ichiro!" just like the Blue Wave fans had done at home.

He's a rookie but nobody here is treating him like a kid coming up. Really, how can we?

—Dan Wilson, Mariners catcher, on Ichiro

Ichiro was making anyone who had doubted his skills eat their words. The player earned the nickname "Wizard" from his teammates, a reference to his amazing, almost magical abilities on the field. At the end of April, he helped to crush the world champion Yankees in a three-game sweep. Ichiro had provided solid defense, on top of getting four hits and one stolen base.

With Ichiro's presence on the team, the Mariners were becoming a force to be reckoned with. The infield—John Olerud, Bret Boone, Carlos Guillen, and David Bell—were working as a tight unit. Ichiro, Mike Cameron, and left fielders Al Martin and Stan Javier were playing solid defense. The pitching staff—Freddy Garcia, Jamie Moyer, Aaron Sele, Paul Abbott, and Ichiro's friend, relief pitcher Kazuhiro Sasaki—along with catcher Dan Wilson were winning games consistently. The team some had predicted would finish third in their division was working together like a well-oiled machine.

At the end of April, the Mariners had a record of twenty wins and five losses. They were the first major-league club in history to pull off twenty wins in April. Ichiro was also named the American League's top rookie for the month. In May, Ichiro continued to impress, helping the Mariners to sweep the Toronto Blue Jays in a three-game series and collecting nine hits in three days. At this point, Ichiro's batting average was approaching .400. By mid-May the Mariners faced the Yankees again. Although they lost the first game, 14–10, Ichiro made a huge running catch in the seventh inning, followed by a double in the eighth. Yankees shortstop Derek Jeter said jokingly to him, "Take it easy, man. That's enough."

But it wasn't enough. As the season progressed, Ichiro kept topping himself. His success came despite the fact that he was still adjusting to all the traveling. The difference in size between Japan and the United States is immense, and moving from hotel to hotel presented some challenges. "The room has to be pitch dark or else I can't get to sleep," Ichiro explained.

As opposed to Japan, where practices before games are intense, Ichiro was surprised at how mild the level of pregame preparation was. "We don't run, we don't do any stretching, just some light batting practice in the batting cage. The rest is up to each individual player. I like to warm up by running up and down the hallway in front of the locker room."

Tossing and Turning

When Ichiro sleeps, he makes sure he changes the side he's lying on constantly. When his wife, Yumiko, asked him why, he replied, "If you always put your weight on one arm and shoulder your body gets out of balance, so even when I'm sleeping I try to avoid that."

Whatever methods he was employing, they were working for Ichiro. He finished the first half of the season with a .347 average and twenty-eight stolen bases. He had 134 hits, sixteen more than anyone else in the league. He was also honored when he was selected for the All-Star game as the league's top vote getter, raking in 3,373,035 votes, more than any rookie in major-league history. Ichiro got a huge boost due to ballots cast for him in Japan. He made the history books when he became the first rookie outfielder since 1964 to make the American League's starting lineup.

The second half of the season was more tiring for Ichiro, probably due to the fact that the U.S. major-league schedule is twenty-seven games longer than the Japanese season. Ichiro ultimately finished the season with a .350 batting average. Even with Ichiro's slight decline in production due to fatigue, the

Mariners continued their winning record through the rest of the season. They won 116 regular-season games, tying the major-league record for most victories in a single season.

Ultimately, the Mariners lost their chance to make it to the World Series when the Yankees defeated them for the league championship title. After losing the first two games of the series, the Mariners made a valiant effort in game three, pulling off a 14–3 win. They just couldn't keep the momentum going, though, and the Yanks won the next two games to finish off the series. Ichiro put up decent numbers, knocking out four hits in eighteen at bats for a .222 batting average.

Even so, Ichiro had plenty to celebrate when the season was over. He was named the American League Rookie of the Year, broke the 200-hit barrier, landed the league's MVP (an honor many thought would go to Oakland's Jason Giambi), and won a Gold Glove (making just one fielding error all year). He was also the first player to lead his league in batting and steals in the same season since Jackie Robinson earned the same honor in 1949.

Chapter Ten

Playing It Cool

With his first season as a U.S. major leaguer under his belt, Ichiro was ready to turn up the heat again in 2002. "It's very simple. Time and time again, Ichiro has been our go-to guy. He hits, we win," fellow outfielder Mike Cameron said about his teammate and friend.

Ichiro often wears sunglasses to protect his eyes from the sun. A myth spread that Ichiro wore sunglasses even to watch TV. Not true, says the slugger. "That is a total lie, never happens."

Ichiro, who had become a style icon with his hip goatee and trademark sunglasses, had proved that he was a triple threat—a stellar hitter, a gifted fielder, and a speedy base runner. Opponents knew that Ichiro could also steal a base at any moment.

Ichiro got off to a red-hot start in the 2002 season, hitting impressively at every game. In one game, he bunted twice for base hits, and in another he made hits down the left-field line and right-field line twice each. His streak came to a brief halt when he cut his left knee while chasing down a foul ball at an April 26 game and had to sit out the next two games. Ichiro had to get four stitches, but he quickly healed.

By April 30, he was back in the lineup for a game against the Chicago White Sox. From then until May 12, he had a twelve-game hitting streak. He got twenty-three hits in forty-nine at bats for an astonishing .469 average. "He came into the league and tore it up, and no one has figured out how to pitch [to] him," teammate Mark McLemore told *Sports Illustrated*. "It's like he's figuring them out."

By June 10, Ichiro had confounded major-league pitchers, who were desperately trying to detect a weakness in him. He was leading the majors in infield hits with twenty-nine for the season, and pitchers were trying to intentionally walk him. Piniella decided that putting Ichiro in the dominant third spot in the batting order for a couple of games would be a good idea. "Now, at least, if they walk him, we'll have the meat of the order up," he explained. Added Boston Red Sox manager Grady Little:

"There's no secret way to get him out. All you can do is concentrate on the other eight guys."

While Ichiro was making baseball look effortless on the field, off the field, he was still struggling with his language skills: "What I don't like is when I'm with my teammates facing the cameras and microphones. I want to go ahead and speak, even if I make mistakes. But once the mike's on me I find I can't say anything." Ichiro still needed an interpreter to communicate with his team. But he was working on his English—and even tried learning some simple Spanish greetings to communicate with some of the Spanish-speaking players on the team.

❝*I think what I did is help to reduce the distance between Japan and America.*❞

—ICHIRO

Ichiro also displayed the kind of pregame focus that most of his teammates weren't used to seeing. Before a game, while his teammates would joke around with one another, Ichiro would go through six different stretches to limber up for the match ahead.

Being a superstar has its drawbacks, namely that other teams' fans want to psych you out. Ichiro had become accustomed to opposing teams' fans berating him in Japanese, calling him names such as *baka* (idiot) and *hetakuso* (lousy). It didn't bother Ichiro, though. In fact, it only fueled him to perform better!

In a July 13 game against Tampa Bay, Ichiro hit two home runs—his first multi-homer game. By the All-Star break, Ichiro had 124 hits under his belt, the second highest in Mariners history. When it came time to choose the league's All-Star team, Ichiro once again led the league with 2,516,016 votes.

But just as easily as a player can be on a hot streak, a slump can follow. In August and September, Ichiro's batting averages were .282 and .248, respectively. It was a difficult time. Rather than slamming home runs and base hits, he was hitting more fly balls. He also cut down his base stealing.

This wasn't the first time in his career that Ichiro had experienced a slump. One reason for Ichiro's slump could have been that like in the previous season, he was battling end-of-season fatigue. But he knew that it was just a matter of time before he got his groove back. To help get to the bottom of it, Ichiro turned inward. "If I'm in a slump, I ask myself for advice," he said.

One baseball scout surmised that Ichiro had hit his "wall," saying, "Ichiro's gassed. His swing has slowed down, and he's bailing out to get to inside pitches." Even Piniella admitted that "we need to rest him more." Ichiro had been driving hard all season, and it had caught up with him.

Baseball writers also suggested that pitchers had worked to wear Ichiro out with pickoff attempts. When he was leading off from first base, pitchers often tried to throw him out. As a result, Ichiro was forced to repeatedly dive back to the base. Throughout the season, the pitchers may have succeeded in sapping some of the dynamite player's energy.

But despite his tough time, pitchers still viewed him as a threat. On September 19, he was walked intentionally for the twenty-sixth time in the season. He broke a team record formerly held by Ken Griffey Jr., who had been intentionally walked twenty-five times in 1993.

66*Ichiro does so many things right at bat, it's scary. He just does it with a unique style.*99

—LOU PINIELLA

Ichiro wasn't the only one struggling with the difficult season. Although the Mariners were in first place in their division on August 18, they won only eighteen of their last thirty-eight games. That left them in third place, ten games out of first. It wasn't enough to make it to the play-offs. The Mariners became the sixteenth team in major-league history to win a total of 300 games over three consecutive seasons without making it to the World Series.

Ichiro didn't feel completely defeated, though. On November 13, he won his second straight American Gold Glove award. He also became the first Mariner ever with two 200-plus-hit seasons and just the sixth player in major-league baseball history with 200-plus hits in his first two seasons. He ended the 2002 season with a .321 batting average.

The first Japanese position player to make it to the U.S. majors had proved that he was more than just a one-season wonder. Ichiro said it better than anyone else could have: "I'm unique. I'm a very rare kind of player." That was no understatement. In fact, he was here to stay.

Chapter | Eleven

Here to Stay

During Ichiro's time off before the 2003 season, he returned to his old stomping grounds and played in the seven-game All-Star series in Tokyo. This time instead of being on the Japanese team, Ichiro was playing for the United States. A lot had changed since his first series against the Americans in 1996.

Ichiro felt very philosophical about everything he had achieved in his first two years in the American major leagues. "Personally, I don't like the term 'success.' It's too arbitrary and too relative a thing. It's usually someone else's definition, not yours," he explained.

In February 2003, Ichiro showed up early to spring training with fresh hopes for his third season in the major leagues. A new manager, Bob Melvin, was on board, replacing Lou Piniella, who had left for Tampa Bay. One of Melvin's mandates was that he wanted to hire utility players like John Mabry so that key hitters like Ichiro could have more days off.

"I'm not a machine. I have learned from whatever happened last year," Ichiro said. "It's very difficult to pinpoint what was the cause of that, but I'm learning from that."

He even joked about the fact that his English hadn't improved much over the break. "Everybody expects me to play better baseball than to speak better in English. So I practice baseball more than practicing better English."

As the season began, the Mariners reinforced that Ichiro was their go-to guy. Despite a slow start (his average in late April was a low .243), Ichiro would prove yet again that he could perform well under pressure.

❝ *Ichiro, from day one, you knew he was something special. He probably has more of a flair than Hideki does.* ❞

—Yankees manager Joe Torre, comparing Ichiro to Japanese left fielder (and Yankee) Hideki Matsui

---

Ichiro's matchup on April 29 against fellow countryman and New York Yankees left fielder Hideki Matsui—known as "Godzilla" to his fans—generated plenty of heat. In his first season with the Yankees, Matsui had become the third Japanese position player (the New York Mets' right fielder Tsuyoshi Shinjo was the second) to make it to the U.S. majors. While Ichiro and Matsui were in Japan, they both enjoyed superstar status. So naturally their U.S. face-off was front-page news in their homeland. One Japanese reporter told the *Seattle Times* that their stepping on the field together "is like the World Series."

Despite all the hoopla, both Japanese superstars only got one hit each in the course of the game, Ichiro scoring a bunt single in the seventh inning, Matsui turning in a ninth-inning single. Though Ichiro didn't have any other hits, his team still benefited from his skills as a top-notch fielder and base runner. "If he doesn't beat you at the plate, he can help you win the game in other ways," manager Melvin said later about his confidence in Ichiro.

Ichiro's so-so performance in the game, in which the Mariners beat the Yankees 6–0, only seemed to make him work harder. By the end of May, he had bumped up his batting average to .389. When the All-Star break rolled around, once again Ichiro made the cut. He was also the American League's top vote getter for the third year in a row.

In late July, he showed off some of his power-hitting abilities. With two outs in the ninth inning of a July 18 game against the Kansas City Royals, Ichiro reached a landmark moment when he scored his first grand slam as a U.S. major leaguer.

With his help, the Mariners clobbered the Royals, 6–3. Then in a July 25 game against the Texas Rangers, Ichiro blasted his tenth home run of the season, the first time in his U.S. major-league career that he hit the double digits in homers.

❝*He does something different every time up. He slaps, he has power, he hits the ball where it's pitched, he'll pull the ball. And with his speed, you don't know what's going to happen.*❞

—ROY HALLADAY, BLUE JAYS PITCHER, ON ICHIRO

Ichiro got a chance to best Matsui on August 10. In another matchup against the Yankees, the Mariners scored an 8–6 win, helped along by Ichiro's two RBIs. His batting average was .336.

While many pitchers had learned to fear Ichiro, it was clear that batters still hadn't learned their lesson. In a mid-August game against the Blue Jays, Ichiro wowed the crowd with another of his trademark throws, recalling his first season with the Mariners. When the Blue Jays' Reed Johnson attempted to go from first to third after teammate Eric Hinske singled to right field, Ichiro ricocheted the ball from right field to third baseman Mark McLemore. A shocked Johnson said, "I saw it, and I thought I could make it to third. I was surprised." Commenting on the speed of Ichiro's throw, Mariners' pitcher Shigetoshi Hasegawa, who once played with Ichiro on the Blue Wave, said, "That throw was faster than my fastball. That was ninety-five, ninety-six miles per hour." He joked, "I think Ichiro should be the closer [closing pitcher]."

Yet by the end of August, Ichiro faced another slump—his monthlong average was .242. "It's not as if I've changed anything with the way I'm moving my body. I guess it is somewhat strange that I'm not hitting," he remarked. "Of course, I have to accept this fact and not make excuses."

With fall in the air, Ichiro seemed to come out from under his doldrums. In a September 5 game against the Baltimore Orioles, Ichiro slammed a two-run homer, helping his team to win 6–4 in a thirteen-inning marathon. Then in a September 20 game against the Oakland A's, Ichiro drove in a career-high five runs. His two-run single in the game's fourth inning made history. Ichiro became one of only three players in major-league history to reach 200 hits in their first three major-league seasons. (The other honorees are Johnny Pesky and Lloyd Waner.) "I cannot express how sincerely happy I am about what I accomplished today," he said.

Ichiro has accomplished so much in his career, all before age thirty. He ended his third season as a major leaguer with a .312 batting average and pulled in 212 hits, sixty-two RBIs, and thirty-four stolen bases. Unfortunately, his batting average fell twenty-six points in the final six weeks of the season. The Mariners were ultimately eliminated in the running for the American League division race, and some baseball observers linked the team's late-season struggles to Ichiro's.

After the season was over, he told a group of reporters, "I had never experienced such pressure. . . . I felt it especially in mid-September, right around the time I was getting to 200 hits." But he still had a lot of hope for the future, saying, "I don't know how to handle it next year, because you can't prepare for that during the off-season. But at least I experienced this year, so it could be huge for next season."

No doubt he'll take the off-season to regroup and refocus his energy. And he'll be back in 2004, working and playing as hard as ever.

Epilogue

A Bright Future

I chiro's success as a U.S. major leaguer gives inspiration to other Japanese ballplayers hoping to find success in the country where baseball was born. Although the idea of a Japanese position player succeeding in America was once a novel concept, Ichiro proved that nonpitchers from his country could be just as fast, just as good, and just as intimidating as their U.S. counterparts. He took a stereotype that existed for years and turned it on its head, paving the way for his fellow countrymen.

After three years playing with the Mariners, Ichiro is now eligible for salary arbitration, a MLB process that allows players to renegotiate their original contract so that their salary reflects their value to the team. Ichiro, who will not be a free agent until 2006, has expressed interest in another three-year contract with the Mariners. You can be sure that Seattle fans are pretty happy about that!

In 2003 Ichiro decided to put his famous name to good use by teaming up with Starbucks and the Make-a-Wish Foundation in Japan. Ichiro donated $25,000 to help in their effort to grant wishes to children with life-threatening medical conditions in Japan.

Along with other baseball heavyweights like Derek Jeter, Sammy Sosa, and Pedro Martinez, Ichiro was selected to participate in a worldwide advertising campaign for American major-league baseball called "I Live for This." The campaign features Ichiro and the other players talking about how much they love the game. In Ichiro's part, he speaks Japanese while English subtitles run at the bottom of the screen.

The ad campaign could be a slogan for Ichiro. After all, Ichiro's talent and love for baseball helped him break the mold and open the door for other Japanese position players to try their fortunes in the United States. He left behind a comfortable career in Japan and risked it all to become a major-league baseball player in America.

Ichiro has won fans around the world. Those who travel to Nagoya, Japan, can even visit a museum Ichiro's father established in his honor. There, among Ichiro's baby shoes and his first retainer, are pictures and memorabilia of him growing up through the years. The museum tells a story about a boy who dreamed big.

This trailblazer, whose talent has transformed the major leagues, never forgets that his modern-day fairy tale started with a young boy's dream. "I had a dream," he has said. "And I made that dream come true."

An American reporter once asked Ichiro if he had a message for fans back in Japan. "Please watch me very closely," he said.

After all, if you blink, you might miss another amazing move from the small player with the blinding speed. Opponents, teammates, and fans have been watching Ichiro very closely for the past three years, and it seems that they'll continue to watch him for many years to come.

PERSONAL STATISTICS

Name:
Ichiro Suzuki

Nickname:
Wizard

Born:
October 22, 1973

Height:
5'9"

Weight:
160 lbs.

Bats:
Left

Throws:
Right

BATTING STATISTICS (JAPAN)

Year	Team	Avg	G	AB	Runs	Hits	2B	3B	HR	RBI	SB
1992	Orix	.253	40	95	9	24	5	0	0	5	3
1993	Orix	.188	43	64	4	12	2	0	1	3	0
1994	Orix	.385	130	546	111	210	41	5	13	54	29
1995	Orix	.342	130	524	104	179	23	4	25	80	49
1996	Orix	.356	130	542	104	193	24	4	16	84	35
1997	Orix	.345	135	536	94	185	31	4	17	91	39
1998	Orix	.358	135	506	79	181	36	3	13	71	11
1999	Orix	.343	103	411	80	141	27	2	21	68	12
2000	Orix	.387	105	395	73	153	22	1	12	73	21
	Totals	.353	951	3,619	658	1,278	211	23	118	529	199

BATTING STATISTICS (U.S.)

Year	Team	Avg	G	AB	Runs	Hits	2B	3B	HR	RBI	SB
2001	SEA	.350	157	692	127	242	34	8	8	69	56
2002	SEA	.321	157	647	111	208	27	8	8	51	31
2003	SEA	.312	159	679	111	212	29	8	13	62	34
	Totals	.328	473	2,018	349	662	90	24	29	182	121

Key: Avg: batting average; G: games; AB: at bats; 2B: doubles; 3B: triples; HR: home runs; RBI: runs batted in; SB: stolen bases

FIELDING STATISTICS (JAPAN)

Year	Team	Pos	PO	A	E
1992	Orix	OF	50	0	0
1993	Orix	OF	34	1	0
1994	Orix	OF	261	10	5
1995	Orix	OF	262	14	2
1996	Orix	OF	277	8	2
1997	Orix	OF	269	7	2
1998	Orix	OF	245	12	3
1999	Orix	OF	196	10	0
2000	Orix	OF	218	5	4
	Total		1,812	67	18

FIELDING STATISTICS (U.S.)

Year	Team	Pos	G	C	PO	A	E	DP	FLD%
2001	SEA	OF	152	344	335	8	1	2	0.997
2002	SEA	OF	152	344	333	8	3	0	0.991
2003	SEA	OF	159	351	337	12	2	4	0.994
	Total		463	1,039	1,005	28	6	6	0.994

Key: Pos: position; G: games; C: chances (balls hit to a position); PO: putouts; A: assists; E: errors; DP: double plays; FLD%: fielding percentage

SOURCES

3–4 Rob Rains, *Baseball Samurais: Ichiro Suzuki and the Asian Invasion* (New York: St. Martin's Press, 2001), 112.

7 Ibid., 12.

7 Ibid., 13.

9–10 Ibid., 17.

12 Jim Allen, interview by Toni Hassan, "Olympic Openers & Japanese Baseball," *The Sports Factor,* Radio National, August 9, 2000.

12 Beech, Hannah, "Changing the Game," *Time Asia,* May 3–10, 1999, 46.

13 Noonan, Tim, "Go West, Young Man," *Time Asia,* April 10, 2000, 46.

13–14 Bechtel, Mark, "Rising Sons," *Sports Illustrated,* April 23, 2001, 36.

15 Narumi Komatsu, *Ichiro on Ichiro: Interviews with Narumi Komatsu,* translated by Philip Gabriel (Tokyo: Shinchosha Publishing, 2002), 122.

16 Ibid., 123.

16 Ibid., 126.

16 Ibid.

18 Ibid., 123.

19 Whiting, Robert, "Around the Horn," *Time,* November 18, 2002, 48.

20 Komatsu, *Ichiro on Ichiro,* 127.

21 Ibid., 129.

21–22 Jim Allen, *Ichiro Magic!* (New York: Kodansha America, 2001), 23–24.

22 Komatsu, *Ichiro on Ichiro,* 129–30.

22 Ibid., 130.

24 Ibid., 133.

26 Ibid., 132.

28 Ibid., 135.

29 Mark Stewart, *Ichiro Suzuki: Best in the West* (Brookfield, CT.: Millbrook Press, 2002), 10.

29–30 Komatsu, *Ichiro on Ichiro,* 136.

30 Allen, *Ichiro Magic!,* 41.

31 Ibid., 44.

32 Komatsu, *Ichiro on Ichiro,* 136.

33 Ibid., 137.

35 Allen, *Ichiro Magic!,* 48.

35 Komatsu, *Ichiro on Ichiro,* 138.

35 Ibid., 137.

36 "A Seeker on the Diamond," *Aichi Voice,* spring 1998, <http://www2.aia.pref.aichi.jp/voice/no8/person-no8-1.html> (January 15, 2004).

36 Komatsu, *Ichiro on Ichiro,* 138.

37 Ibid., 139.

38 Ibid., 140.

39 Ibid., 140.

39 Matt Christopher, *At the Plate with . . . Ichiro* (New York: Little, Brown, 2003), 22–23.

41–42 Komatsu, *Ichiro on Ichiro,* 140.

42 Ibid., 141.

43 Ibid.

43 Ibid., 142.

44 Ibid., 141.

44 Ibid.

44–45 Ibid., 144.

45 Ibid., 145.

47 Ibid., 147.

47 Ibid.

48 Ibid., 145.

49 Farber, Michael, "Rising Son," *Sports Illustrated,* December 4, 2000, 68.

49 Stewart, *Ichiro Suzuki,* 20.

50 Farber, Michael, "Rising Son," *Sports Illustrated,* December 4, 2000, 68.

51 Allen, *Ichiro Magic!,* 70.

51 Komatsu, *Ichiro on Ichiro,* 80.

53 Ibid., 148.

53–54 Ibid., 149.

54 Stewart, *Ichiro Suzuki,* 23.

54 Komatsu, *Ichiro on Ichiro,* 152.

55 Christopher, *At the Plate with . . . Ichiro,* 27.

55 Noonan, Tim, "The Magical Mystery Tour," *Time Asia,* November 23, 1998, 32.

56 Komatsu, *Ichiro on Ichiro,* 80.

56 Stewart, *Ichiro Suzuki,* 24.

56 Christopher, *At the Plate with . . . Ichiro,* 28.

57 Ibid., 29.

58 Chass, Murray, "Majors Are Scrambling for Japanese Outfielder," *New York Times,* November 2, 2000, D1.

59 Stewart, *Ichiro Suzuki,* 24.

60 Komatsu, *Ichiro on Ichiro,* 81–82.

60–61 Ibid., 83.

61 Ibid., 84.

62 Ibid., 86.

63 Ibid., 161–62.

63 Ibid., 163.

64 Ibid., 152.

65 Ibid., 153–54.

66 Ibid., 154.

66 Ibid., 88.

68 Christopher, *At the Plate with . . . Ichiro,* 33.

68 Ibid., 4.

69 Ibid., 37.

70–71 Ibid., 38.

71 Rains, *Baseball Samurais,* 109.

72 Pearlman, Jeff, "Big Hit," *Sports Illustrated,* May 28, 2001, 34.

73 Nightengale, Bob, "Far East Stars Rise in West," *USAToday.com,* March 13, 2001, <http://www.usatoday.com/sports/bbw/2001-03-14/2001-03-14-specialichiro.htm> (January 15, 2004).

73 Pearlman, Jeff, "Big Hit," *Sports Illustrated,* May 28, 2001, 34.

73 Christopher, *At the Plate with . . . Ichiro,* 42.

74 Ibid., 42–43.

74 Ibid., 43.

75 Komatsu, *Ichiro on Ichiro,* 25.

76 Rains, *Baseball Samurais,* 115.

77 Komatsu, *Ichiro on Ichiro,* 120.

78 Christopher, *At the Plate with . . . Ichiro,* 65.

78 Komatsu, *Ichiro on Ichiro,* 30.

78 Ibid., 24.

79 Ibid., 149.

81 Pearlman, Jeff, "Seattle Mariners," *Sports Illustrated,* October 22, 2001, 44.

81 Finnigan, Bob, "Zen and the Art of Ichiro," *Seattle Times,* July 8, 2001, <http://archives.seattletimes.nwsource.com/cgi-bin/texis.cgi/web/vortex/display?slug=ichi08&date=20010708> (January 15, 2004).

82 Cannella, Stephen, "Inside Baseball," *Sports Illustrated,* June 10, 2002, 101.

82 Ibid.

83 Price, S. L., "The Ichiro Paradox," *Sports Illustrated,* July 8, 2002, 50.

83 Komatsu, *Ichiro on Ichiro,* 50.

83 Whiting, Robert, "Around the Horn," *Time Asia,* November 18, 2002, 48.

84 Ibid.

84 Cannella, Stephen, "Inside Baseball," *Sports Illustrated,* September 23, 2002, 89.

84 Ibid.

85 Finnigan, Bob, "Zen and the Art of Ichiro," *Seattle Times,* July 8, 2001, <http://archives.seattletimes.nwsource.com/cgi-bin/texis.cgi/web/vortex/display?slug=ichi08&date=20010708> (January 15, 2004).

86 Price, S.L., "The Ichiro Paradox," *Sports Illustrated,* July 8, 2002, 50.

87 Whiting, Robert, "Around the Horn," *Time Asia,* November 18, 2002, 48.

88 Associated Press, "Happy Ichiro Makes Early Return," *ESPN.com,* February 14, 2003, <http://espn.go.com/mlb/news/2003/0214/1509084.html > January 15, 2004).

88 Ibid.

88 Blum, Ronald, "Matsui Faces Suzuki for First Time in Majors," *katu.com,* May 1, 2003, <http://www.katu.com/sports/story.asp?ID=57027> (January 15, 2004).

89 Klapisch, Bob, "Matsui Presents Kinder, Gentler Godzilla," *ESPN.com,* April 30, 2003, <http://espn.go.com/mlb/columns/klapisch_bob/1546943.html > (January 15, 2004).

89   Kurkjian, Tim, "Patience Has Its
      Reward for Ichiro," *ESPN.com,* May
      28, 2003, <http://espn.go.com/mlb
      /columns/kurkjian_tim/1559908
      .html > (January 15, 2004).
90   Poiley, Joel, Schwarz, Alan, Keith,
      Ted, and Northrop, Michael, "Fear
      Factor: Baseball's Most Intimidating
      Players," *Sports Illustrated for Kids,*
      May 2003, 44B.
90   Hickey, John "Ichiro Jolts Jays:
      Spectacular Throw Lifts Mariners,"
      Seattle Post-Intelligencer, August 13,
      2003, D1.
91   Ibid.
91   "Matsui 1–5 as Yankees Down Red
      Sox," *Japan Economic Newswire,*
      September 1, 2003, <http://www
      .japantoday.com/gidx/news271214
      .html> (September 1, 2003).
91   McCauley, Janie, "Mariners Pressing
      Athletics, Red Sox," *USAToday.com,*
      September 20, 2003, <http://www
      .usatoday.com/sports/baseball
      /games/2003-09-20-mariners
      -athletics_x.htm> (January 21,
      2004).
92   Hickey, John, "Pressure Got to
      Ichiro," *Seattle Post-Intelligencer,*
      September 30, 2003, D1.
95   Stewart, *Ichiro Suzuki,* 46.
95   "Happy to Be a Mariner, Ichiro
      Starts New Trend," *Seattle Union
      Record,* December 1, 2000, <http://
      www.unionrecord.com/sports
      /display.php?ID=461> (January 15,
      2004).

BIBLIOGRAPHY

Books

Allen, Jim. *Ichiro Magic!* New York: Kodansha America, 2001.

Christopher, Matt. *At the Plate with . . . Ichiro.* New York: Little, Brown, 2003.

Komatsu, Narumi. *Ichiro on Ichiro: Interviews with Narumi Komatsu.* Translated by Philip Gabriel. Tokyo: Shinchosha Publishing, 2002.

Rains, Rob. *Baseball Samurai: Ichiro Suzuki and the Asian Invasion.* New York: St. Martin's Press, 2001.

Savage, Jeff. *Ichiro Suzuki.* Minneapolis: Lerner Publishing Group, 2003.

Stewart, Mark. *Ichiro Suzuki: Best in the West.* Brookfield, CT: Millbrook Press, 2002.

Selected Newspaper, Magazine, and Online Articles

Bechtel, Mark. "Rising Sons." *Sports Illustrated,* April 23, 2001, 36.

Beech, Hannah. "Changing the Game." *Time Asia,* May 3–10, 1999, 46.

Farber, Michael. "Rising Son." *Sports Illustrated,* December 4, 2000, 68.

Finnigan, Bob. "Zen and the Art of Ichiro." *Seattle Times,* July 8, 2001 <http://archives.seattletimes.nwsource.com /cgi-bin/texis.cgi/web/vortex/display?slug=ichi08&date =20010708> (January 15, 2004).

Hickey, John. "Ichiro Jolts Jays: Spectacular Throw Lifts Mariners." *Seattle Post-Intelligencer,* August 13, 2003, D1.

Kurkjian, Tim. "Patience Has Its Reward for Ichiro." ESPN.com, May 28, 2003 <http://espn.go.com/mlb/columns /kurkjian_tim/1559908.html> (January 15, 2004).

Nightengale, Bob. "Far East Stars Rise in West." *USAToday.com,* March 13, 2001 <http://www.usatoday.com/sports/bbw /2001-03-14/2003-03-14-specialichiro.htm> (January 15, 2004).

Noonan, Tim.
   "Go West, Young Man." *Time Asia,* April 10, 2000, 46.
   "The Magical Mystery Tour." *Time Asia,* November 23, 1998, 32.

Pearlman, Jeff. "Big Hit." *Sports Illustrated,* May 28, 2001, 34.

Price, S. L. "The Ichiro Paradox." *Sports Illustrated,* July 8, 2002, 50.

Whiting, Robert. "Around the Horn." *Time Asia,* November 18, 2002, 48.

WEBSITES

Seattle Mariners: The Official Site

www.mariners.org

This is a great resource for everything there is to know about Ichiro's team, from stats to career highlights.

Jim Allen's Japanese Baseball Page

www.2.gol.com/users/jallen/jimball.html

The sportswriter and Japanese baseball expert gives a comprehensive view of the history of Japanese baseball.

Michiyo's Sports Info Japan

www.t3.rim.or.jp/~sports/index.html

Get educated about Japanese sports with this site, which includes detailed information about Ichiro's days with the Orix Blue Wave.

Aichi Voice

www.2.aia.pref.aichi.jp/voice/no8/person-no8-1.html

An online publication of the Aichi prefecture, Ichiro's home region, it includes features about the baseball player.

INDEX

A

Abbot, Paul, 77
Aiko-Dai Meiden High
    School, 21, 25
Allen, Jim, 12
Anaheim Angels, 69
Asahi Shimbun, 7

B

Baltimore Orioles, 91
Barfield, Jesse, 58
Baseball Magazine, 30
Bell, David, 76–77
Bonds, Barry, 44, 48
Boone, Bret, 77
Boston Red Sox, 82
Bross, Terry, 45

C

Cameron, Mike, 3, 74, 77,
    81
Chiba Lotte Marines, 14, 43,
    67
Chicago White Sox, 7, 82
Chunichi Dragons, 17, 19,
    28
Cleveland Indians, 55

D

Dai Nippon, 8
Dai Tokyo, 8
DiMaggio, Joe, 10
Doi, Shozo, 29–32, 35

E

Ebisu, Nobuyuki, 55

F

Fukura, Junichi, 38

G

Garcia, Freddy, 77
Garciaparra, Nomar, 55
Giambi, Jason, 3, 80
Griffey, Ken Jr., 56, 71, 85
Guillen, Carlos, 3, 77

H

Halladay, Roy, 90

Hankyu, 8
Hargrove, Mike, 55
Harimoto, Isao, 46
Hasegawa, Shigetoshi, 38,
    91
Hassan, Toni, 12
Heid, Ted, 10
Hentgen, Pat, 48
Hernandez, Ramon, 75–76
Hilo Stars, 34–35
Hinske, Eric, 90
Hiraoka, Hiroshi, 6
Hiroshima, 9
Hoshino, Nobuyuki, 55
Hudson, Tim, 2

I

Irabu, Hideki, 13, 43, 67

J

Japanese Professional
    Baseball League, 8, 10
Javier, Stan, 77
Jeter, Derek, 78, 94
Johnson, Randy, 71–73
Johnson, Reed, 90
Jongewaard, Roger, 57

K

Kaisei Gakko school, 5
Kansas City Royals, 89–90
Kawamura, Kenichiro,
    32–33
Kintetsu Buffaloes, 31, 36
Komatsu, Tatsuo, 19
Konishi, Keizo, 72
Koshien, 24–26
Kyodo News Service, 72

L

Little, Grady, 82
Long, Terrence, 75–76
Los Angeles Dodgers, 13,
    49, 69

M

Mabry, John, 88
MacArthur, Douglas, 9
Make-a-Wish Foundation, 94

Martin, Al, 74, 77
Martinez, Edgar, 3
Martinez, Pedro, 48, 94
Mathews, T. J., 2–3
Matsui, Hideki, 88, 90
Matsuzaka, Daisuke, 62
McLemore, Mark, 82, 90
Mecir, Jim, 3
Melvin, Bob, 87, 89
Miwata, Katsutoshi, 29
Moyer, Jamie, 55–56, 77
Murakami, Masanori, 11, 13

N

Nagasaki, 9
Nagoya Kinko, 8
Nagoya Stadium, 17
Nakamura, Go, 21–22
Nankai Hawks, 11
Neel, Troy, 54
New York Mets, 14, 49, 69,
    89
New York Yankees, 8, 13,
    67, 78, 80, 88–90
Nippon Ham Fighters, 46,
    62
Nishiguchi, Fumiya, 53
Nishizaki, Yukihiro, 61
Nomo, Hideo, 13, 31, 36, 49

O

Oakland A's, 2–3, 75–76, 80,
    91
Ogawa, Hirofumi, 38
Ogi, Akira, 35–36, 63, 67
Okamoto, Ayako, 19
Olerud, John, 3, 77
O'Malley, Tom, 45
Orix Blue Wave, 2, 28–32,
    35, 38–39, 42–48,
    50–51, 54–55, 57,
    59–61, 63, 66–69
Ortiz, Jose, 3
Osaka Tigers, 8

P

Palmeiro, Rafael, 76
Pearl Harbor, 9
Pesky, Johnny, 91

Piazza, Mike, 48–49
Piniella, Lou, 56, 73–75,
    84–85, 87

R
Ripken, Cal Jr., 48
Robinson, Jackie, 80
Rodriguez, Alex, 71
Ruth, Babe, 8

S
Safeco Field, 1, 70
San Diego Padres, 73
San Francisco Giants, 11
Sasaki, Kazuhiro, 3, 13, 69,
    77
Sato, Yoshinori, 38
Schilling, Curt, 55
Seattle Mariners, 1–3, 13,
    55–57, 69–73, 75–78,
    80, 85, 88–90, 92–93
Seattle Post-Intelligencer, 76
Seattle Times, 76, 89
Seibu Lions, 38, 45, 61–62
Sele, Aaron, 77
Shibaura Club, 8
Shimbashi Athletic Club
    Athletics, 6
Shinjo, Tsuyoshi, 89
Shinozuka, Kazunori, 18
Shoriki, Matsutaro, 7
Sosa, Sammy, 55, 94
Sports Illustrated, 82
Suzuki, Ichiro, 65, 94–95
    batting statistics, 97
    birth and childhood,
    15–20
    fielding statistics, 98
    high school baseball,
    21–26
    Hilo Stars, 34–35
    Japanese Professional
    baseball, 27–33, 36–67
    personal statistics, 96
    Seattle Mariners, 1–4,
    70–93
    US Major League
    baseball, 67–69
Suzuki, Nobuyuki, 2, 15–20,
    28
Suzuki, Yoshie, 15

Suzuki, Yumiko Fukushima,
    53–54, 64–65, 67,
    69–71, 79

T
Taguchi, So, 35, 41
Tampa Bay Devil Rays, 84,
    87
Texas Rangers, 13, 75, 76,
    90
Time magazine, 12
Tokyo Senators, 8
Toronto Blue Jays, 78, 90
Torre, Joe, 88

V
Valentine, Bobby, 14, 49

W
Waner, Lloyd, 91
Wilson, Dan, 77
Wilson, Horace, 5
World War II, 8–9

Y
Yakult Swallows, 45
Yokohama Country Club, 6
Yomiuri Giants, 8, 11, 18,
    47–48
Yomiuri Shimbun, 8
Yonamine, Wally, 46